Coloring Book Quotes are from:

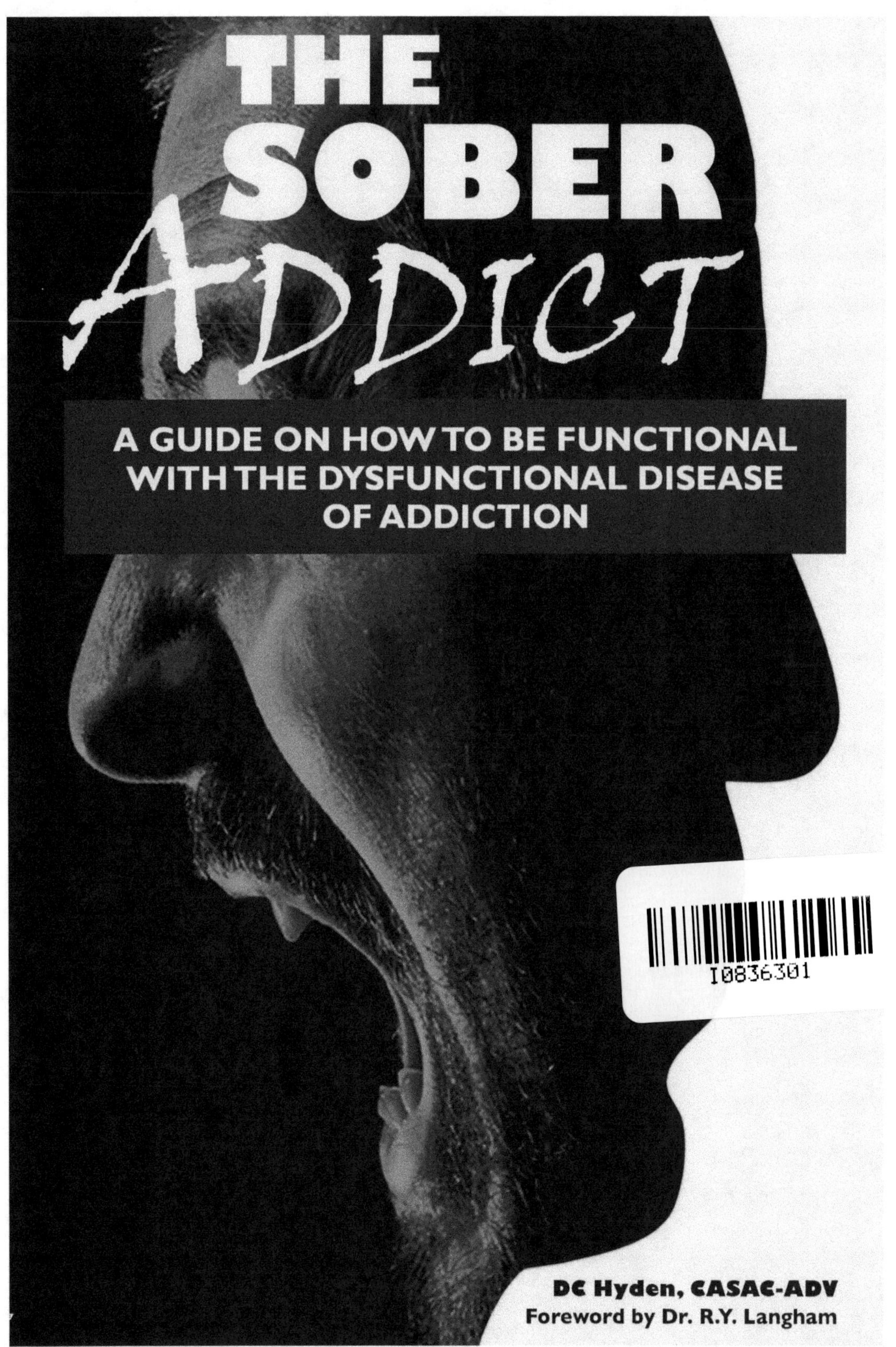

This BooK Belong's To:

Motivational Recovery Quotes
Adult Coloring Book

Published in the United States of America by Hyden Enterprises LLC
New York, New York
Library of Congress Cataloging-in-Publication Data
Hyden, Daniel, [April 2024]
The Sober Addict:
Includes index.
ISBN 978-1-7359738-1-4
Hyden Enterprises
Printed in the United States of America
First Edition

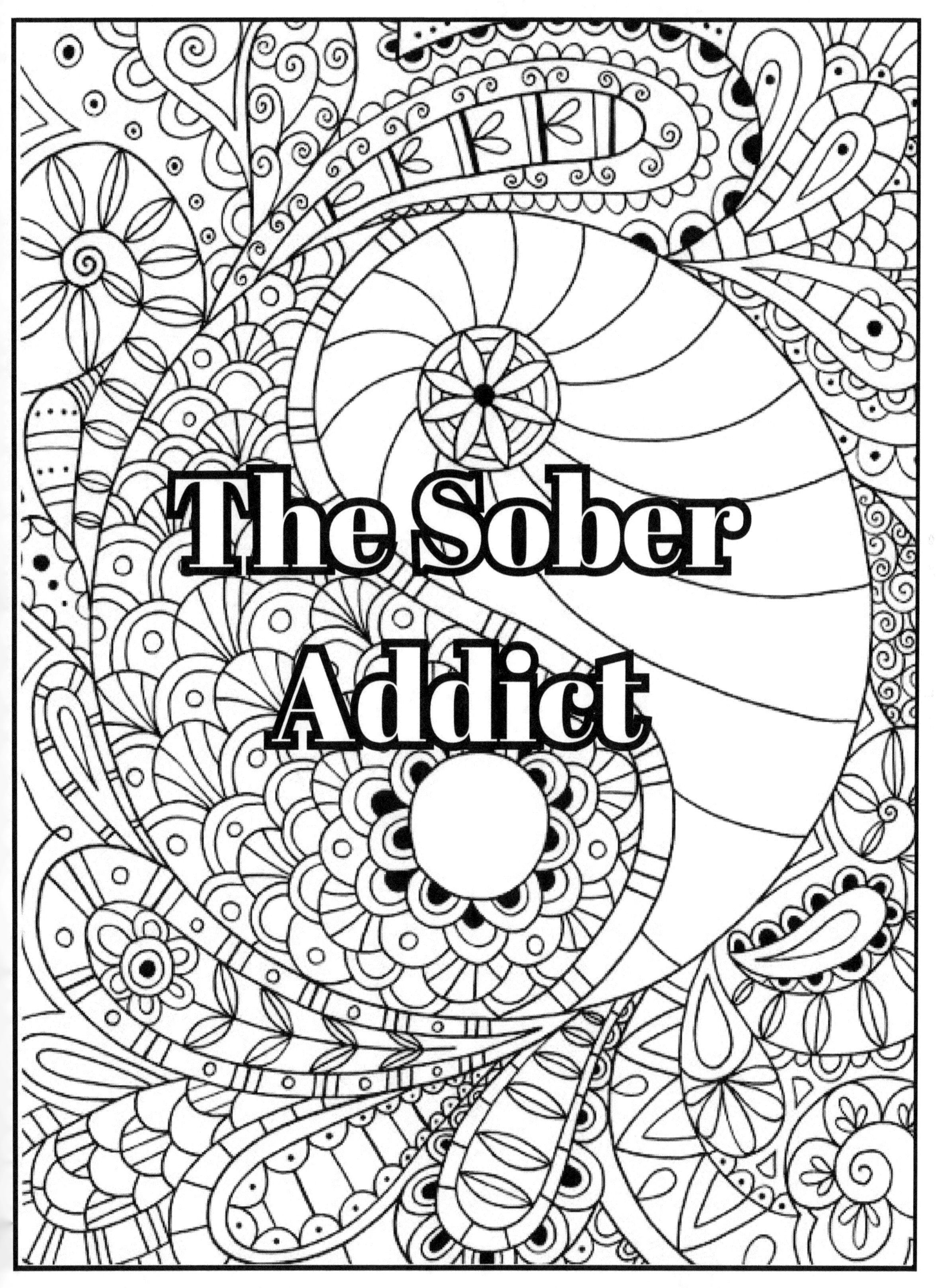
The Sober
Addict

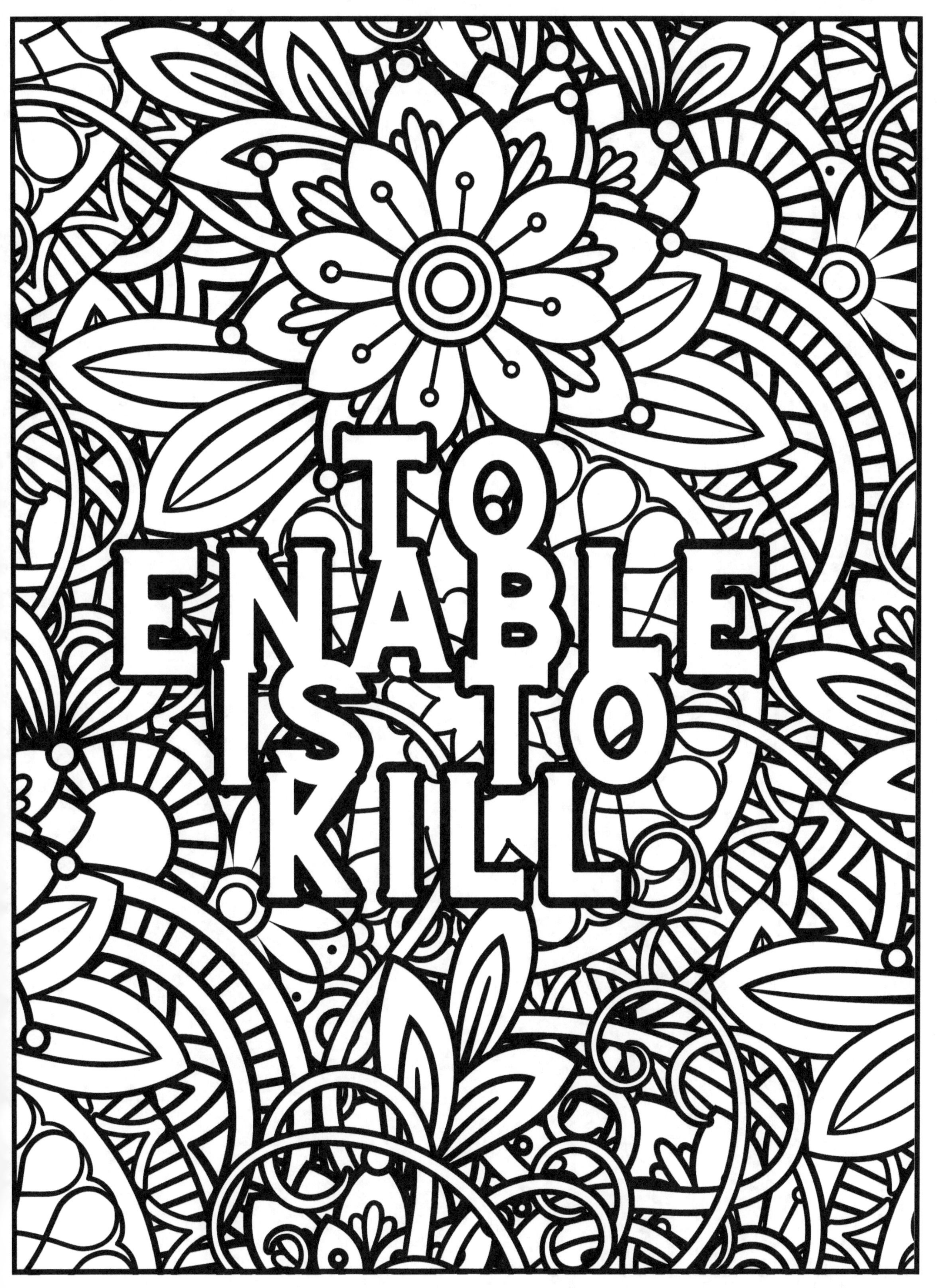
TO
ENABLE
IS TO
KILL

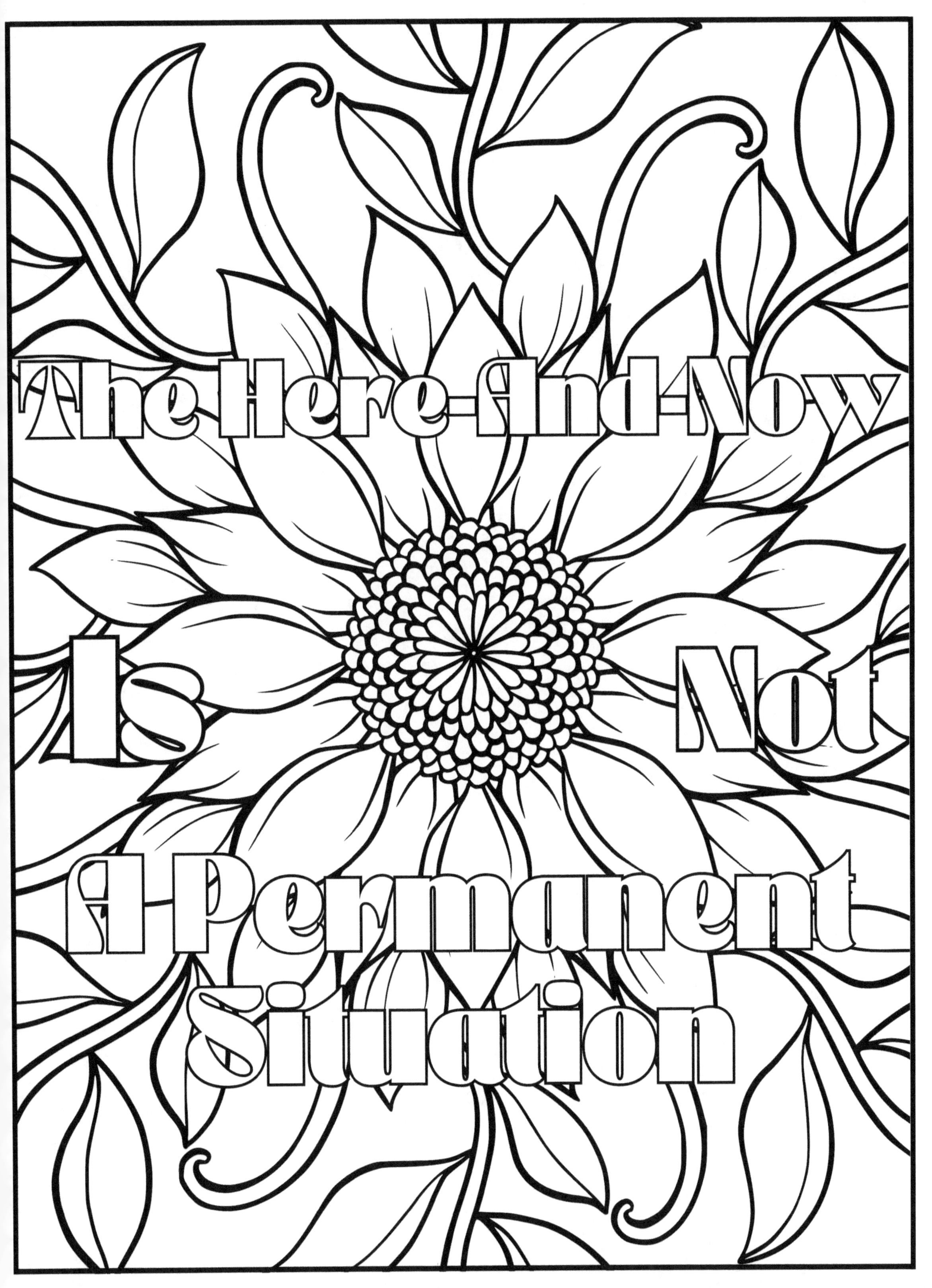
The Here And Now
Is Not
A Permanent
Situation

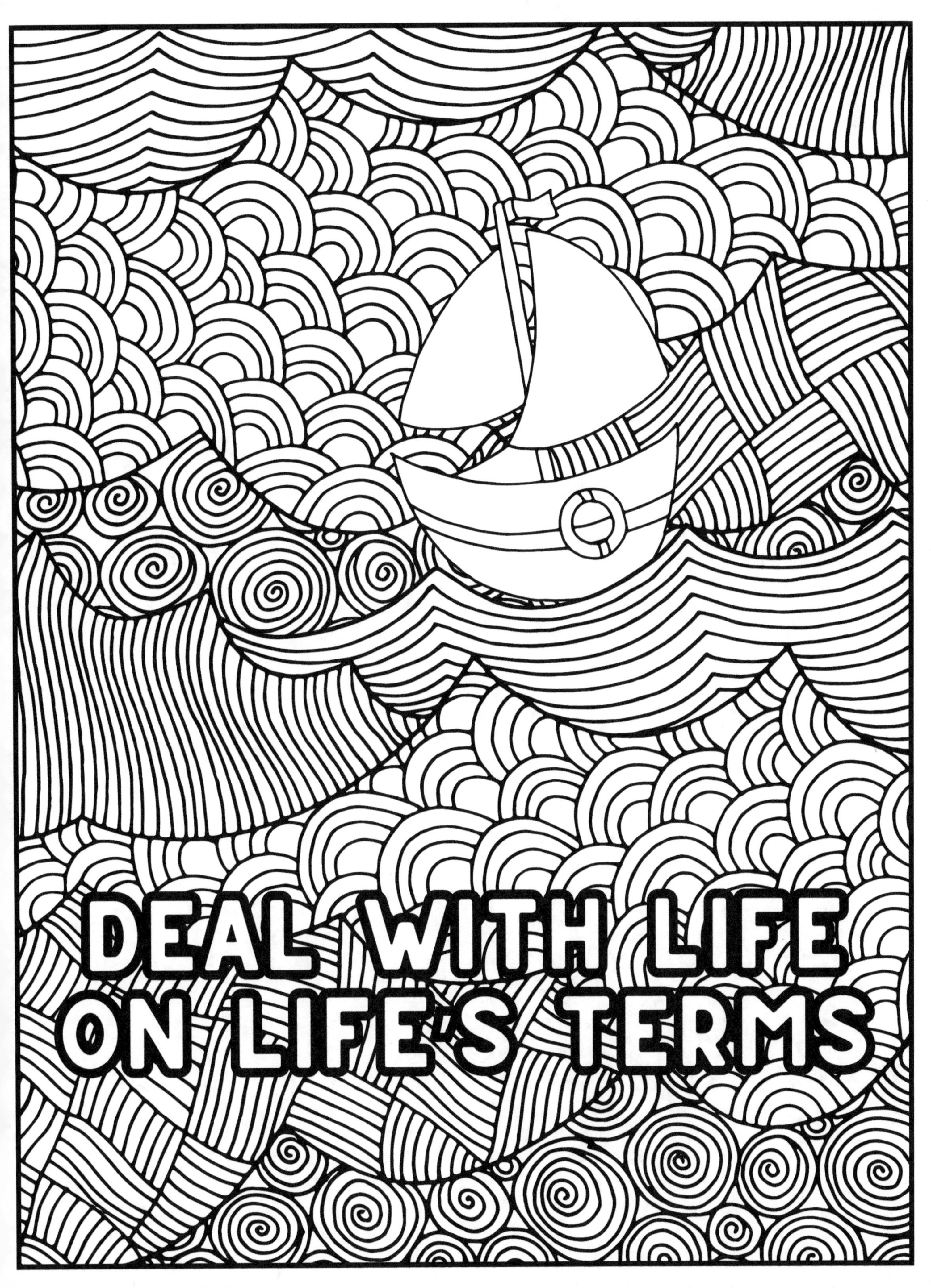
DEAL WITH LIFE
ON LIFE'S TERMS

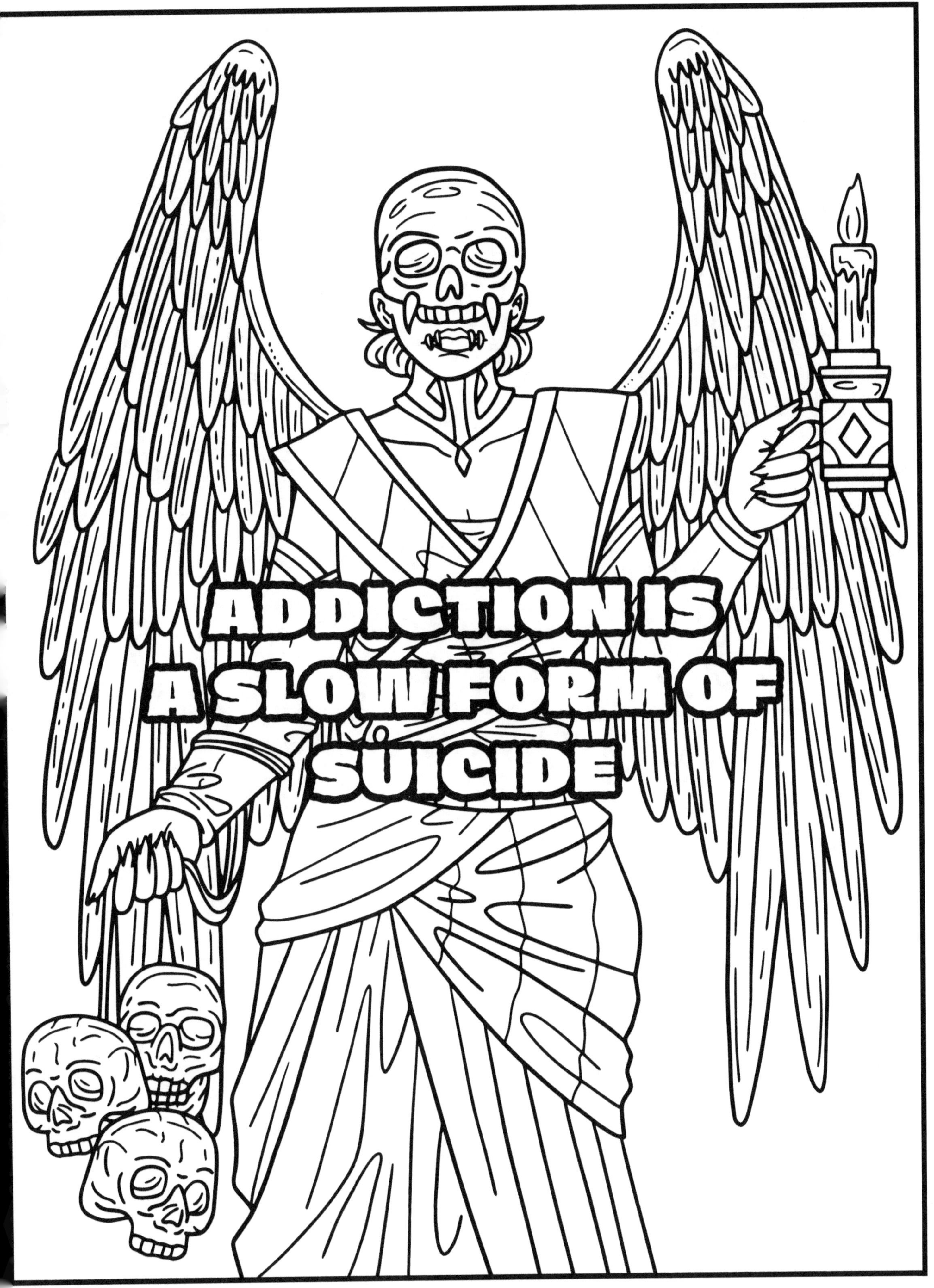
ADDICTION IS
A SLOW FORM OF
SUICIDE

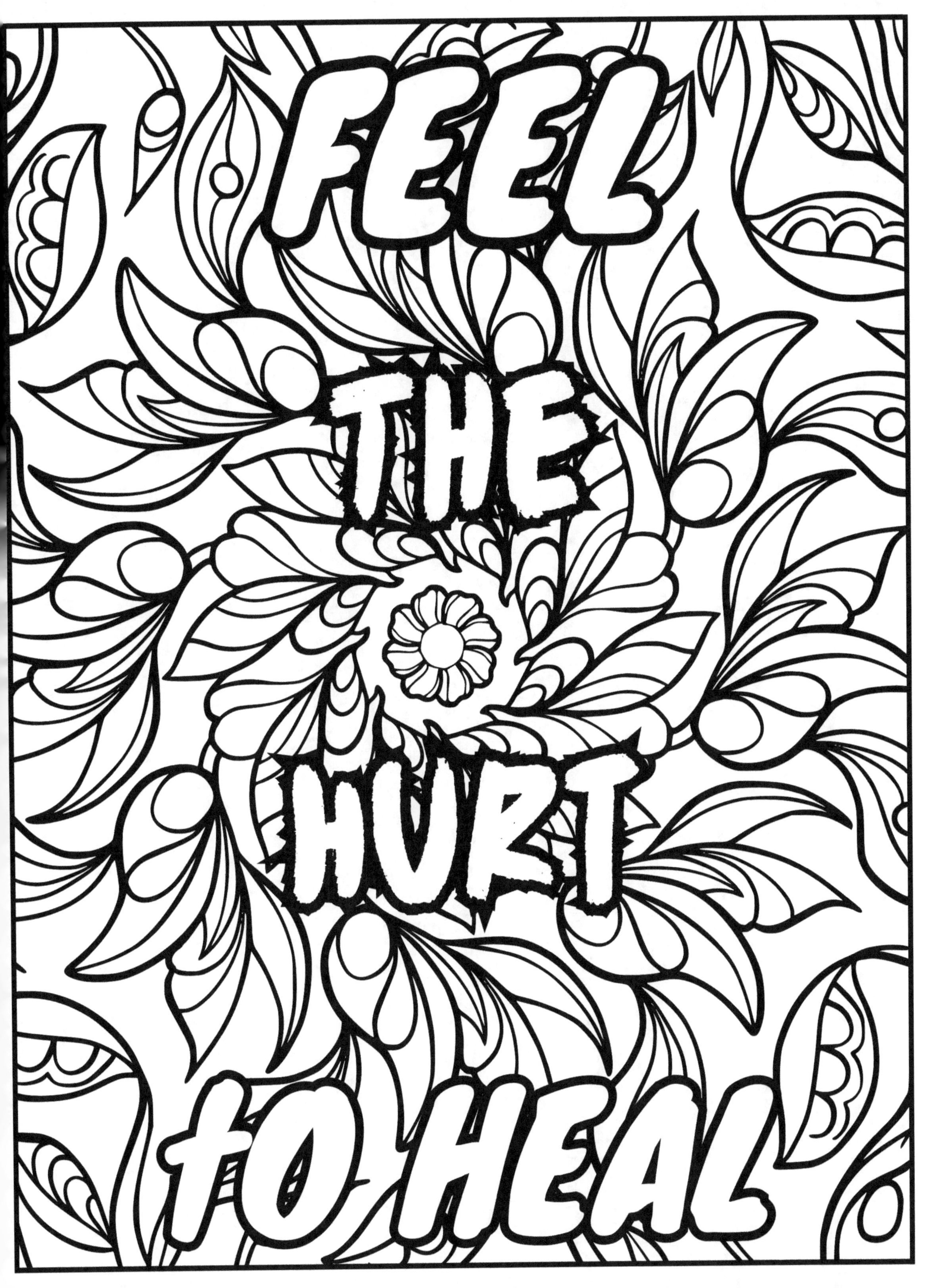
FEEL
THE
HURT
to HEAL

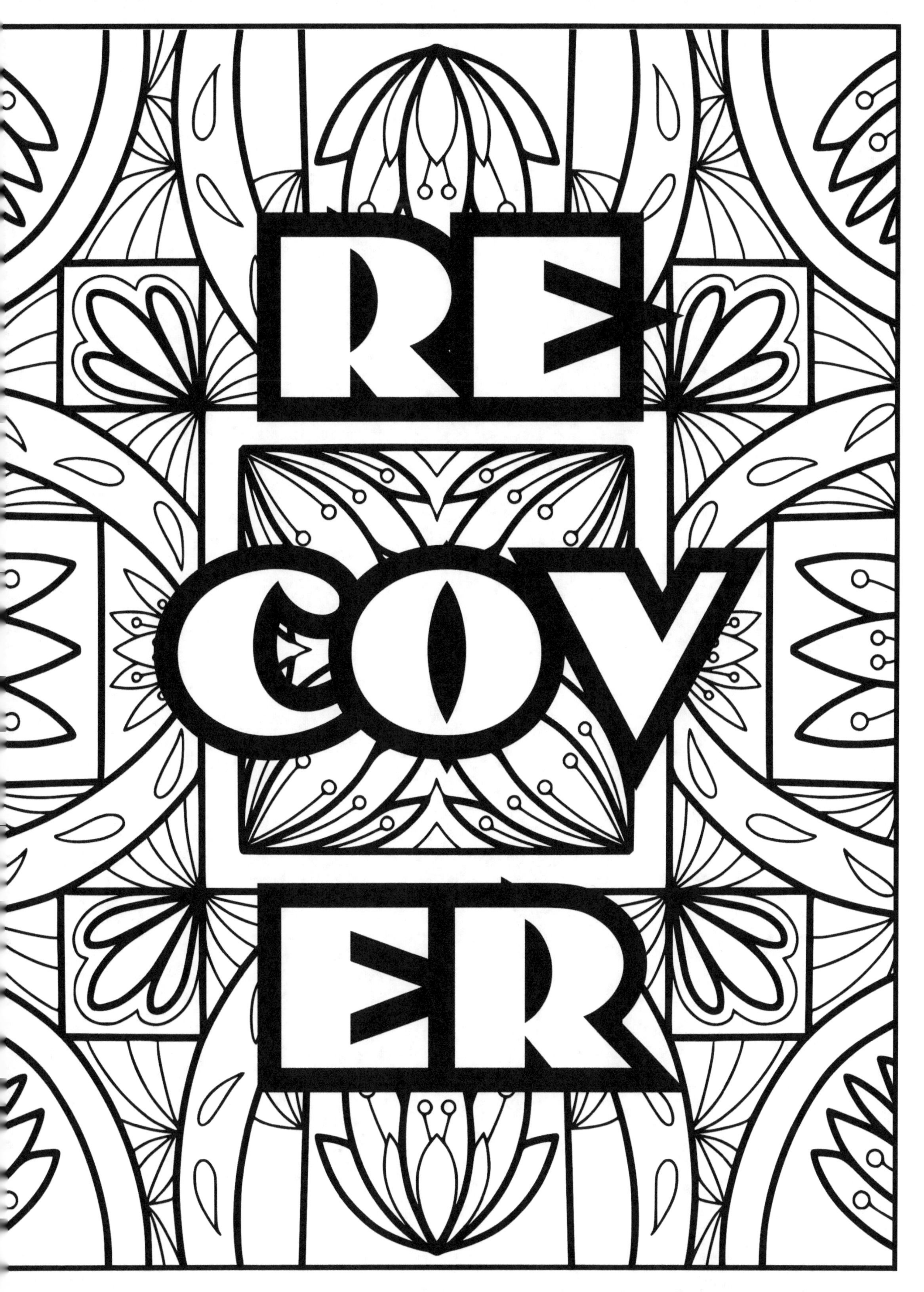
RE
COV
ER

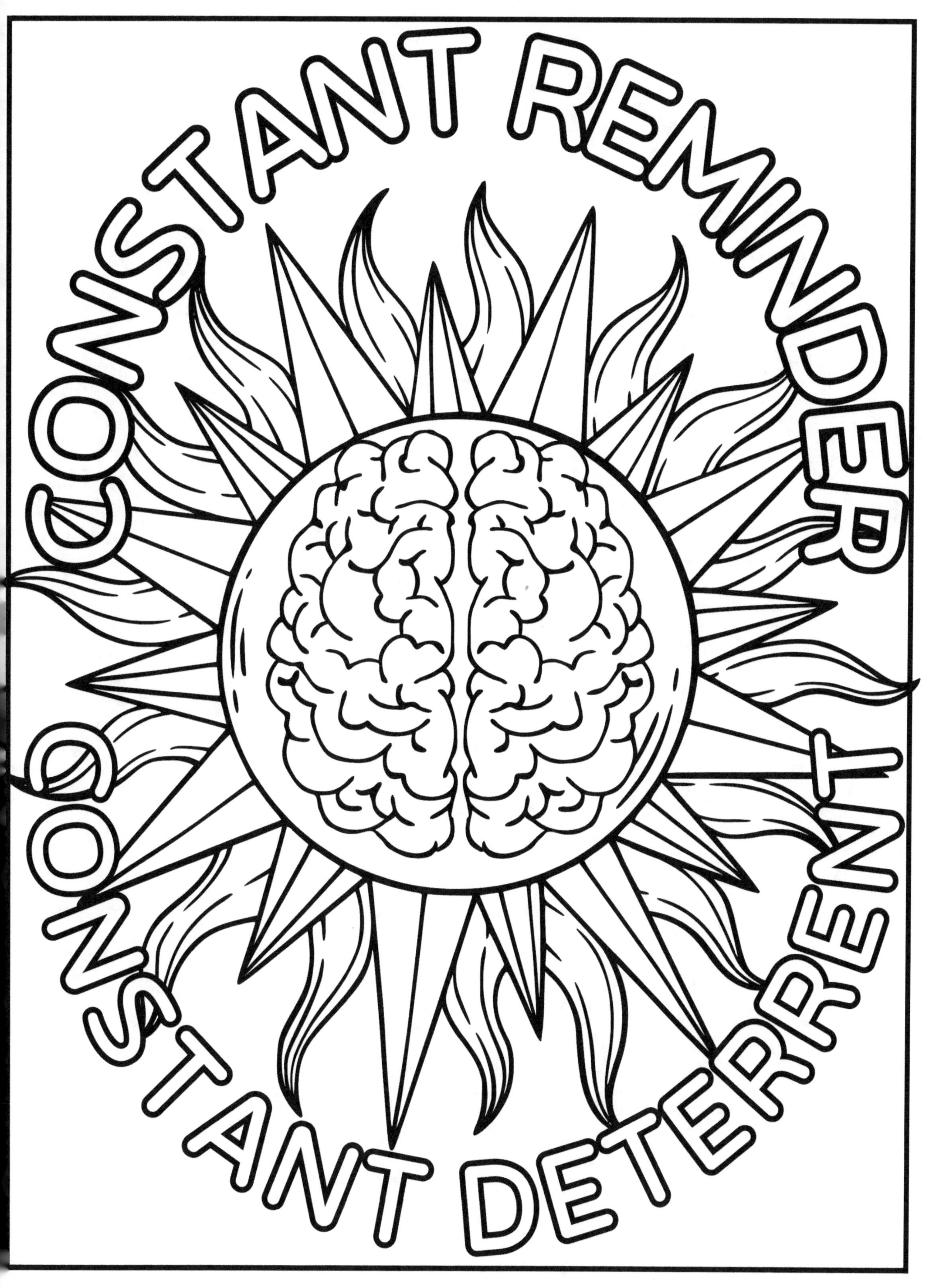
CONSTANT REMINDER
CONSTANT DETERRENT

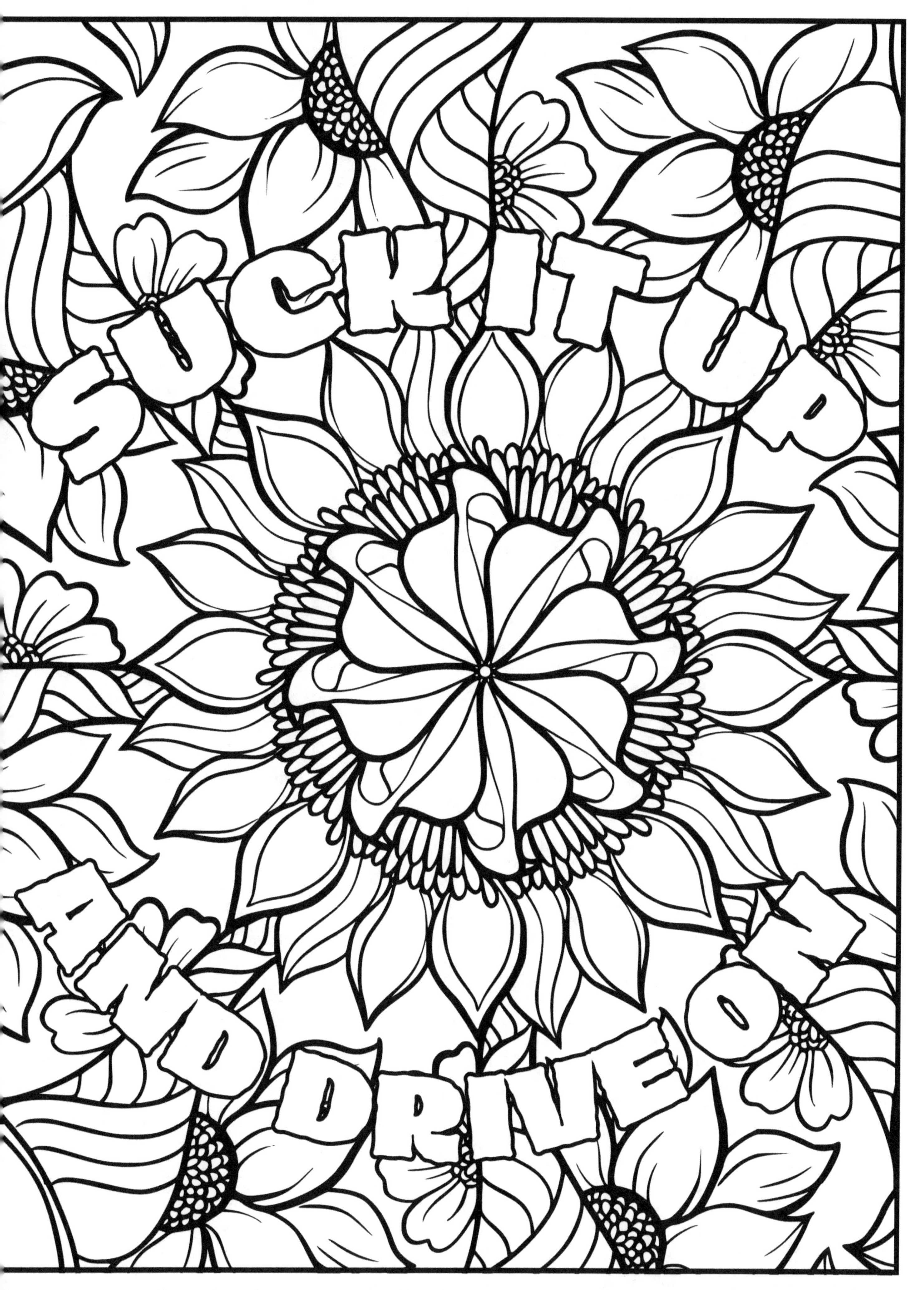
SUCK IT UP
AND DRIVE ON

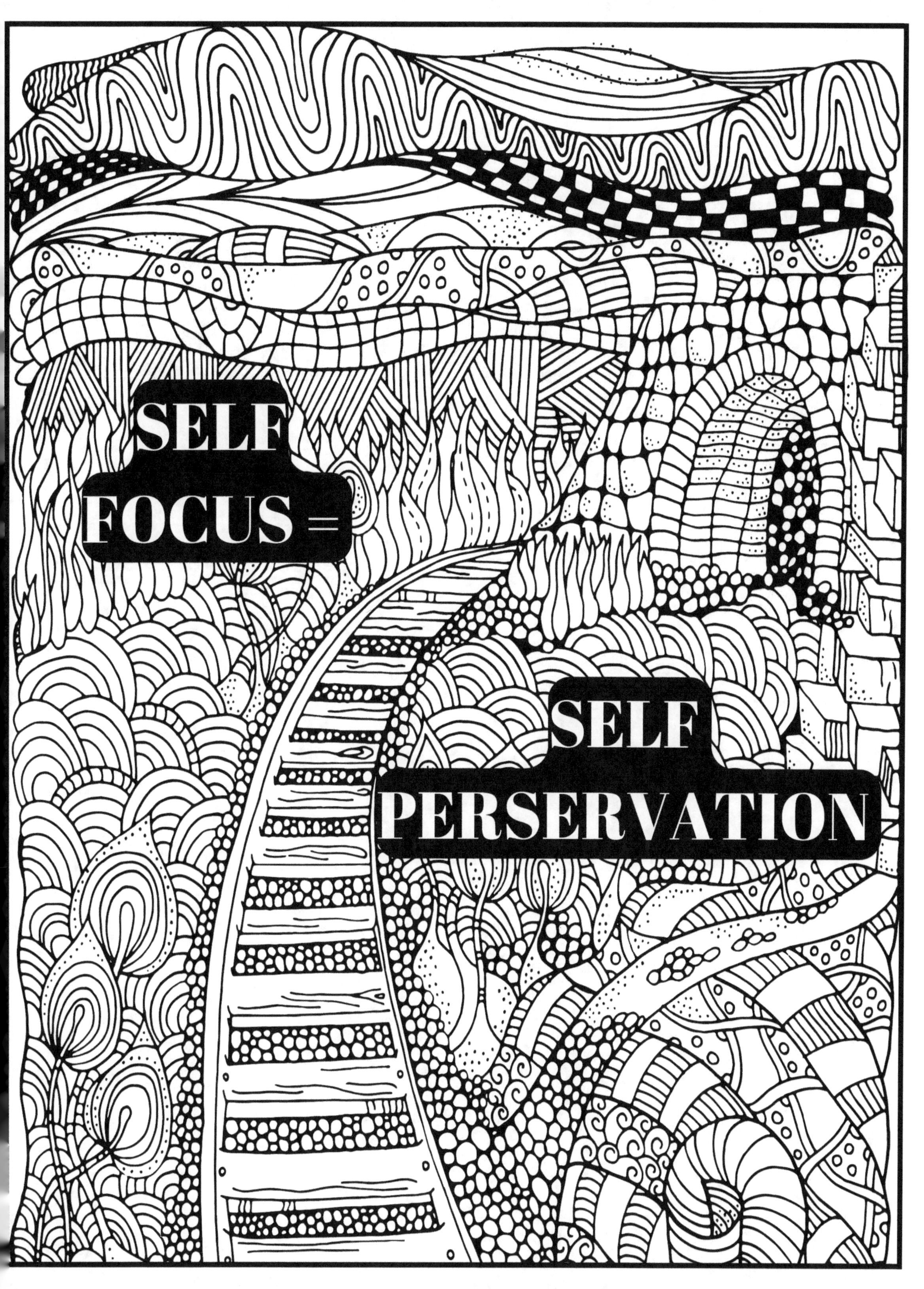
SELF
FOCUS =
SELF
PERSERVATION

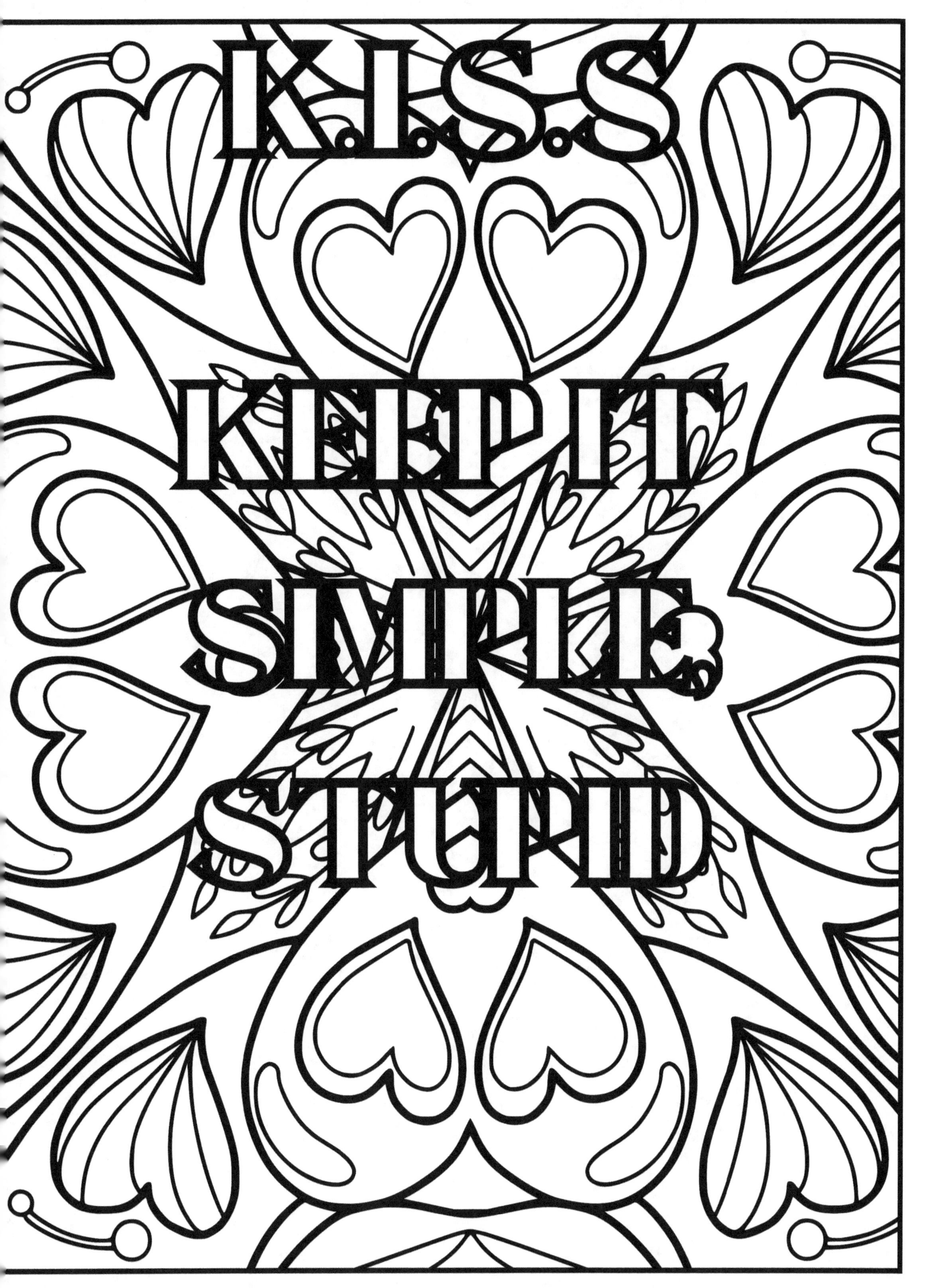
K.I.S.S
KEEP IT
SIMPLE
STUPID

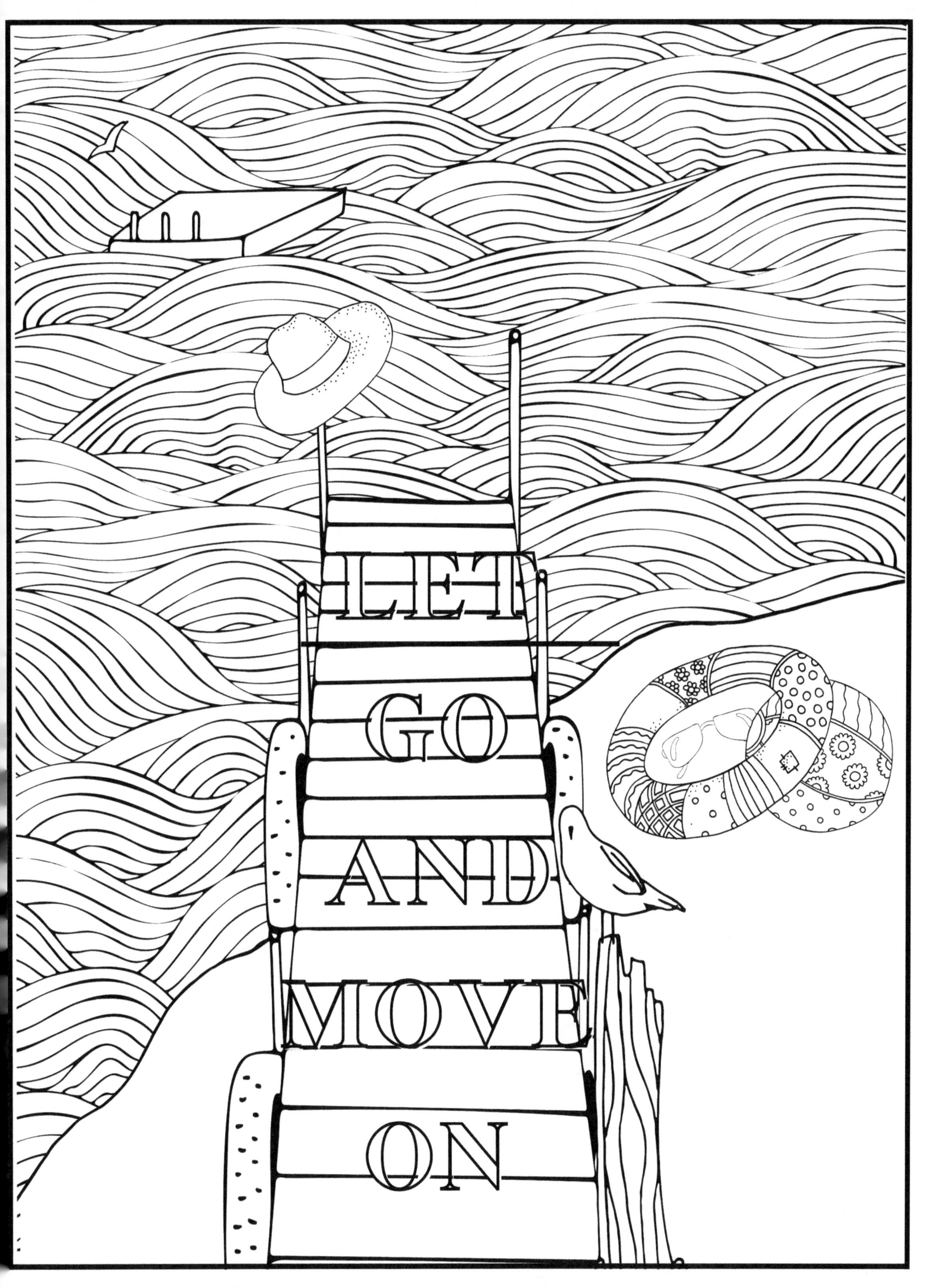
LET
GO
AND
MOVE
ON

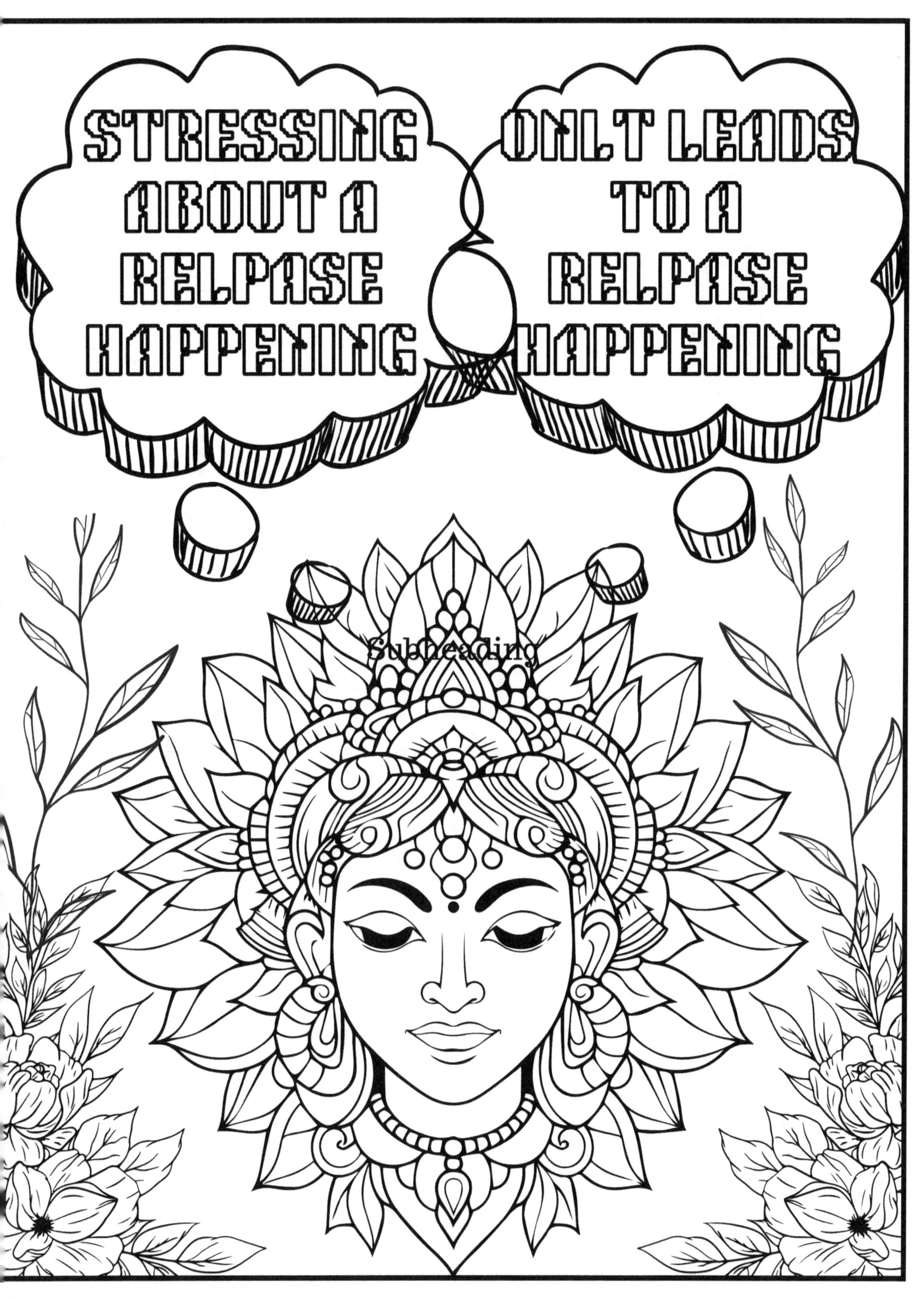
STRESSING ABOUT A RELPASE HAPPENING
ONLT LEADS TO A RELPASE HAPPENING
Subheading

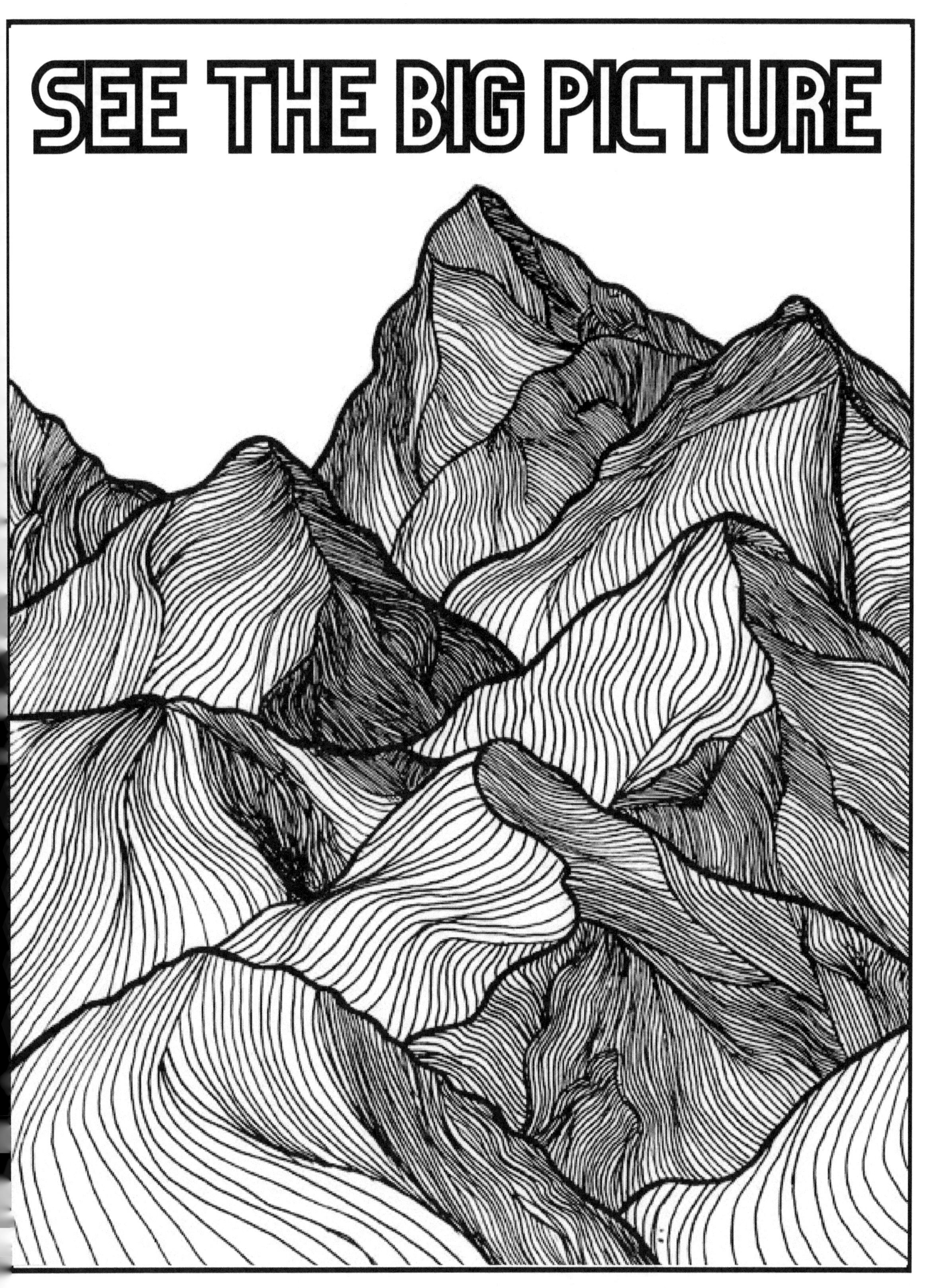
SEE THE BIG PICTURE

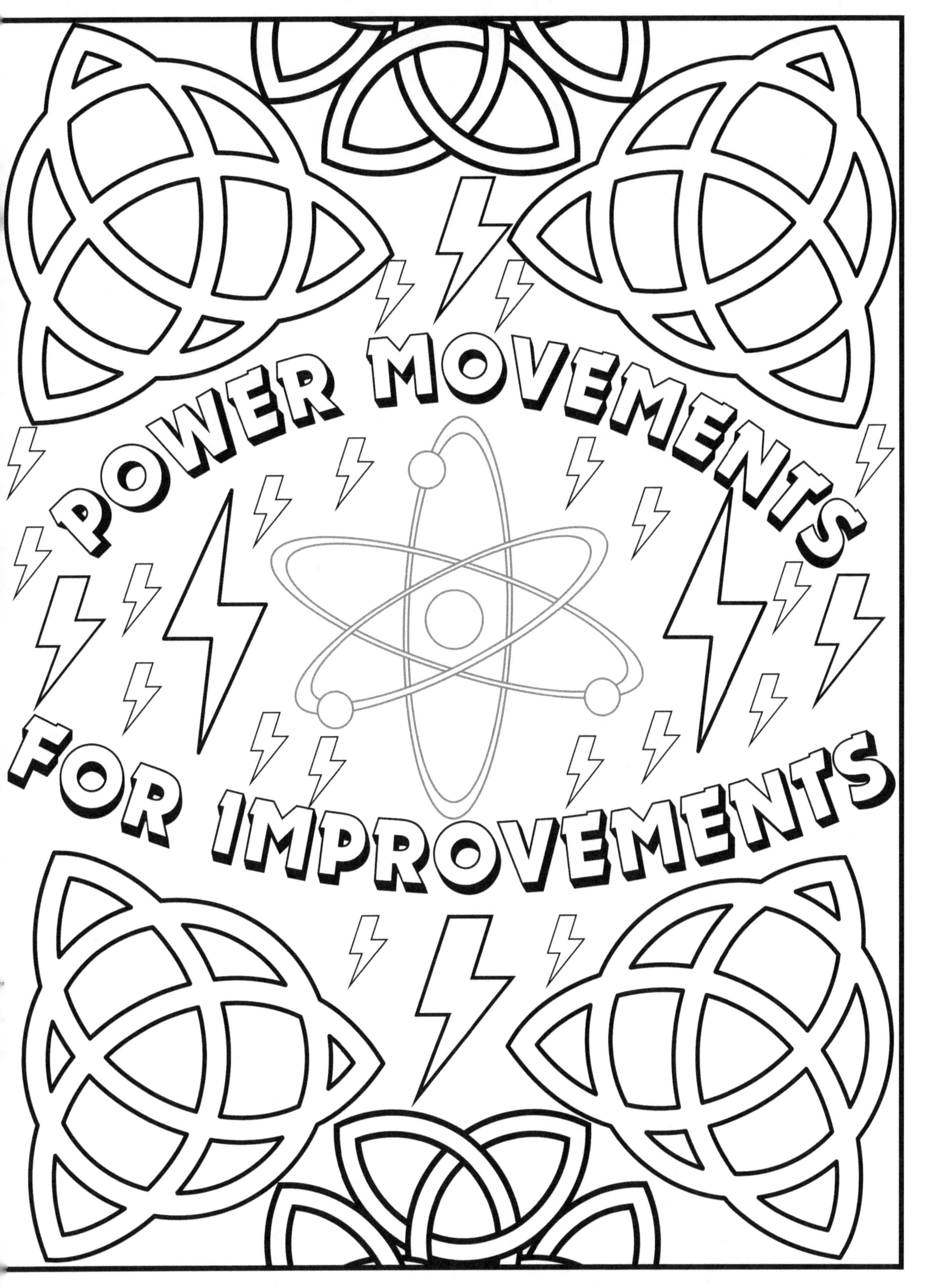
POWER MOVEMENTS
FOR IMPROVEMENTS

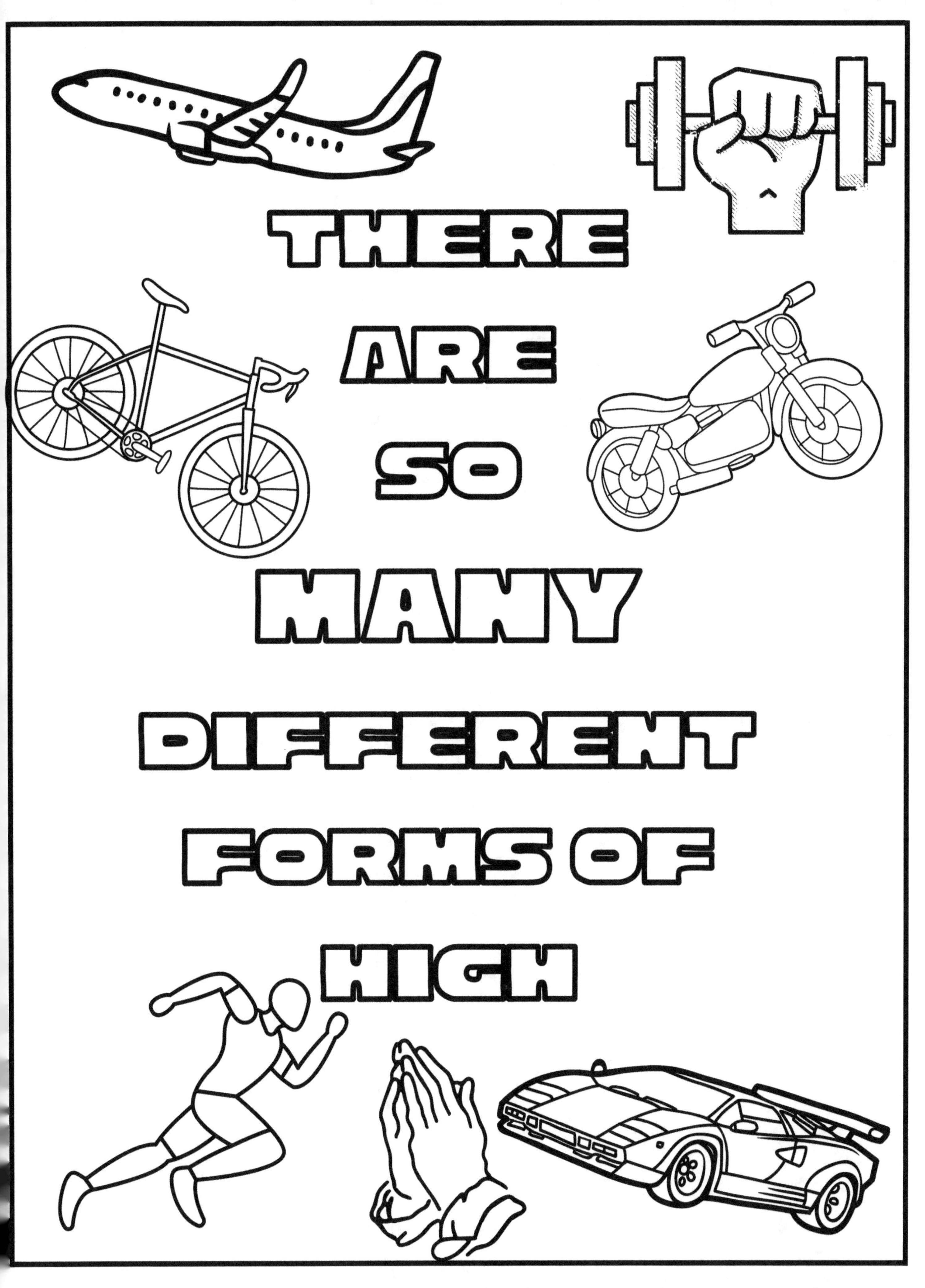
THERE
ARE
SO
MANY
DIFFERENT
FORMS OF
HIGH

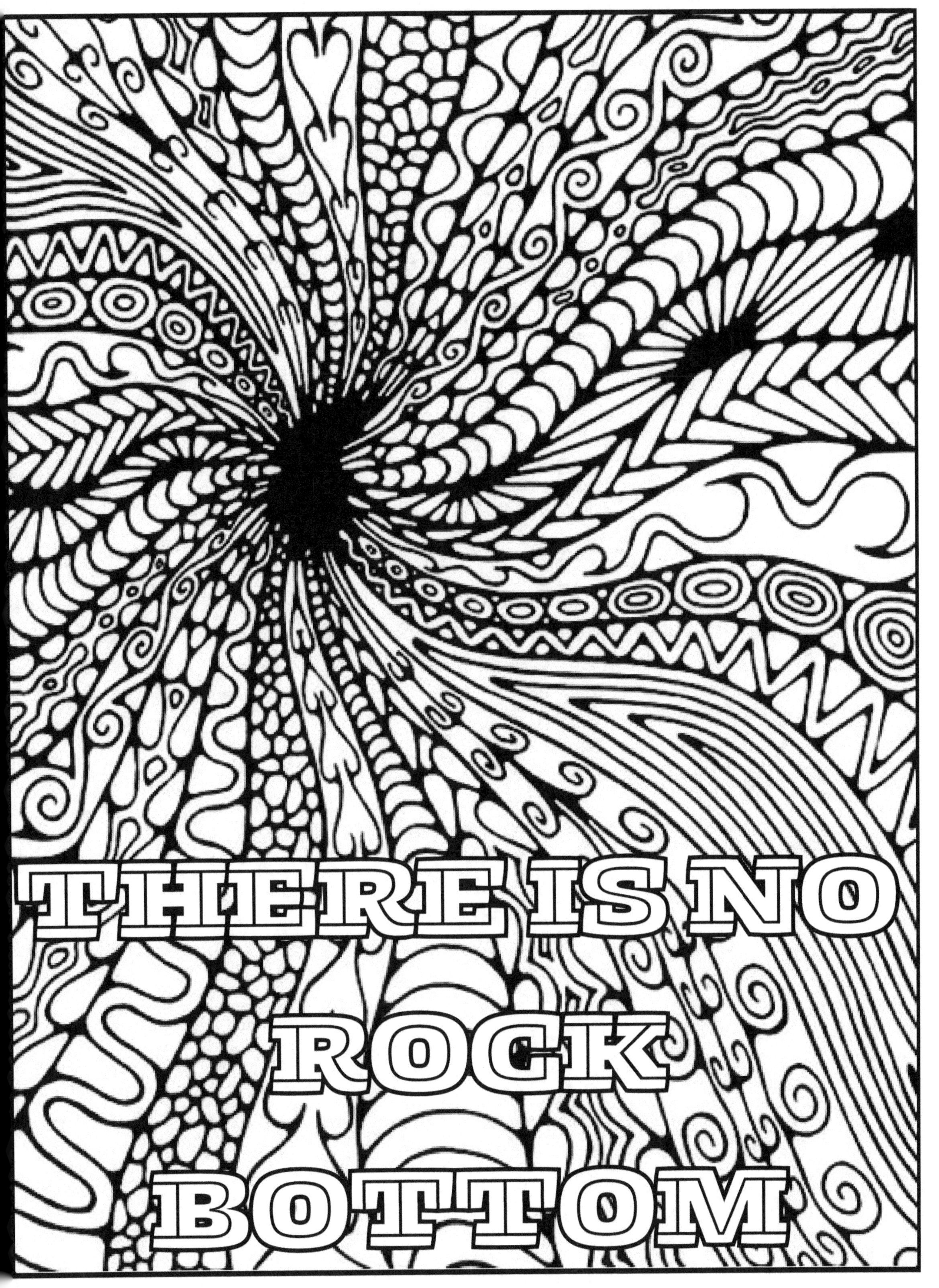
THERE IS NO
ROCK
BOTTOM

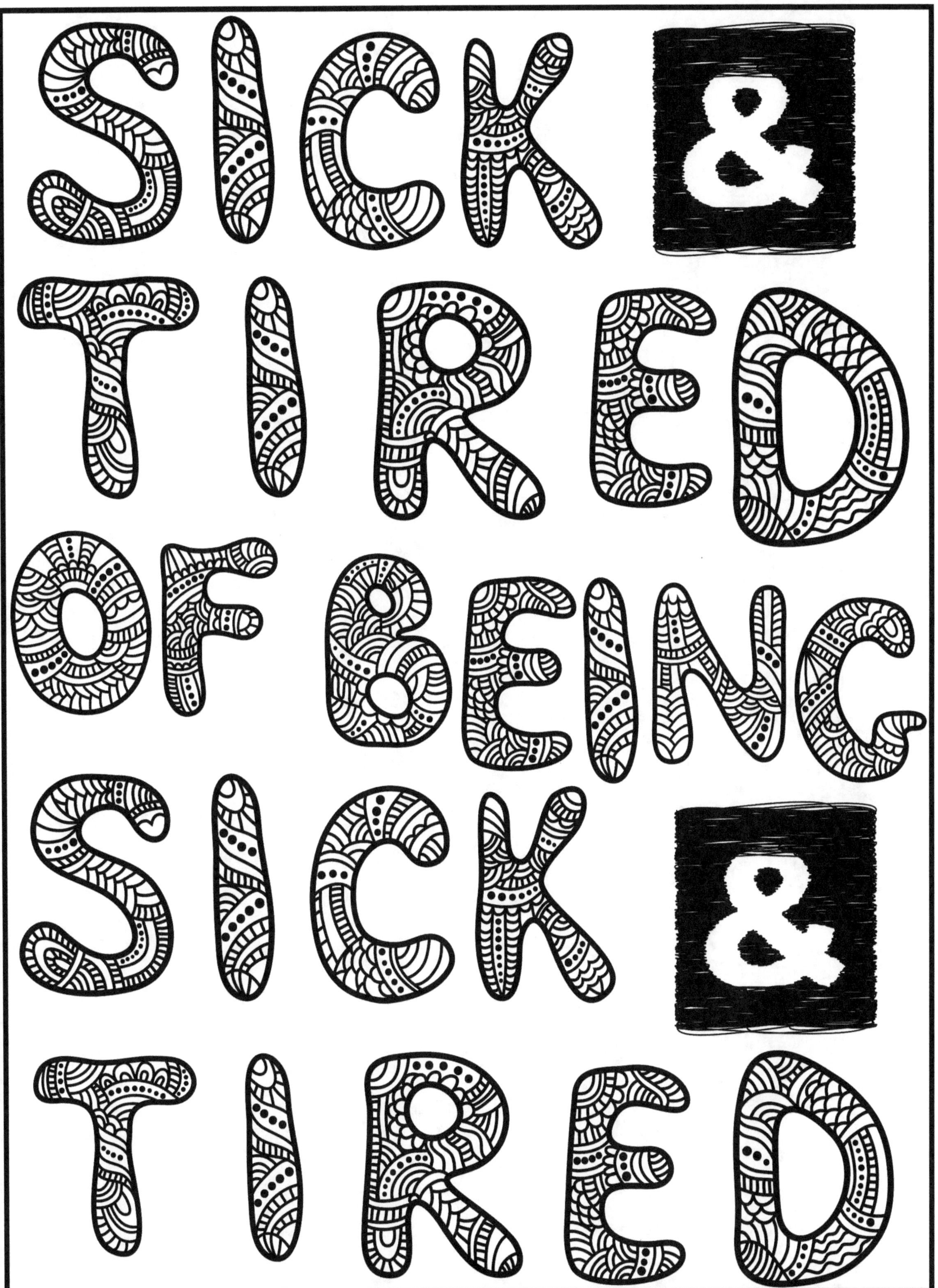
SICK &
TIRED
OF BEING
SICK &
TIRED

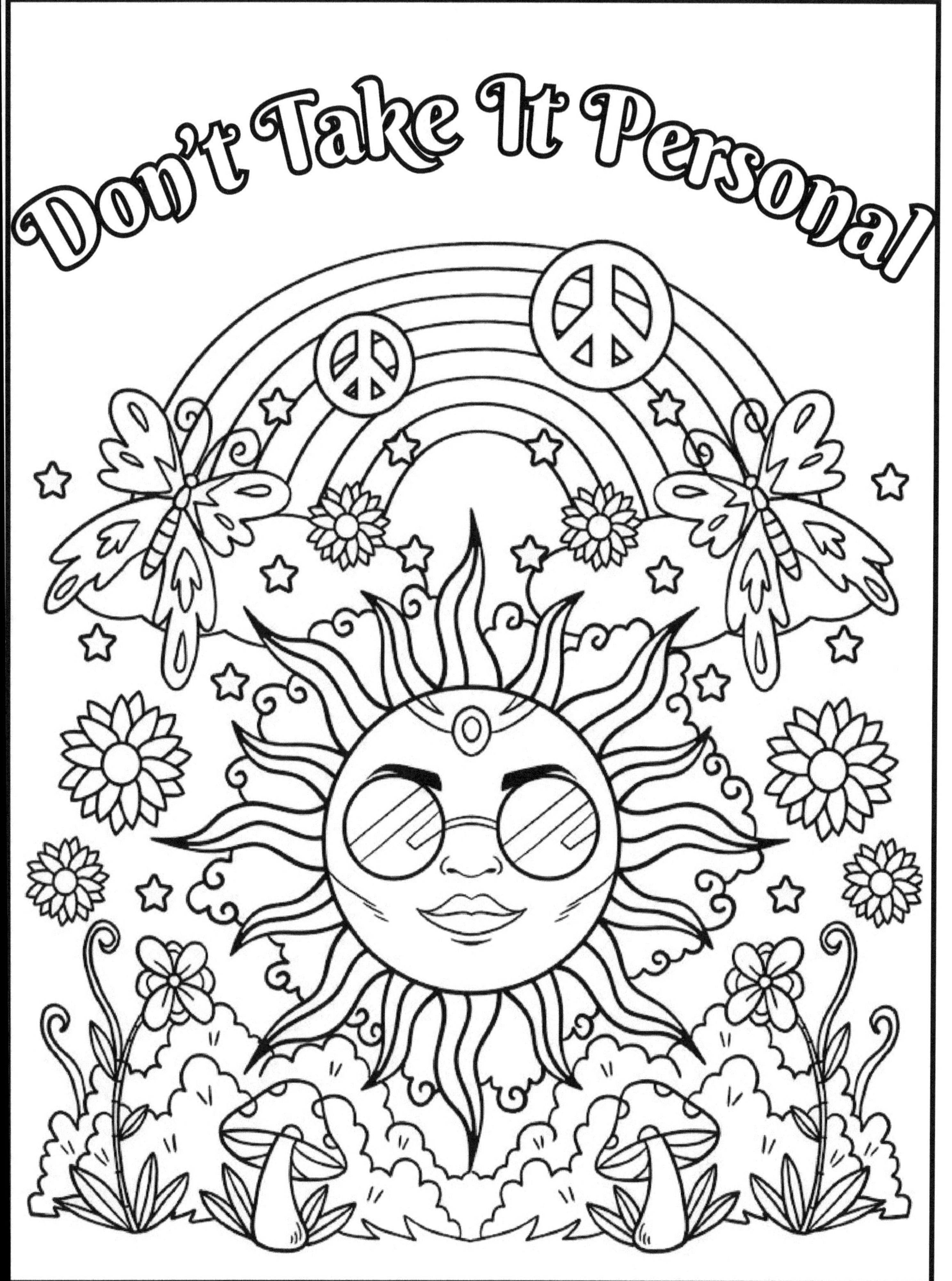
Don't Take It Personal

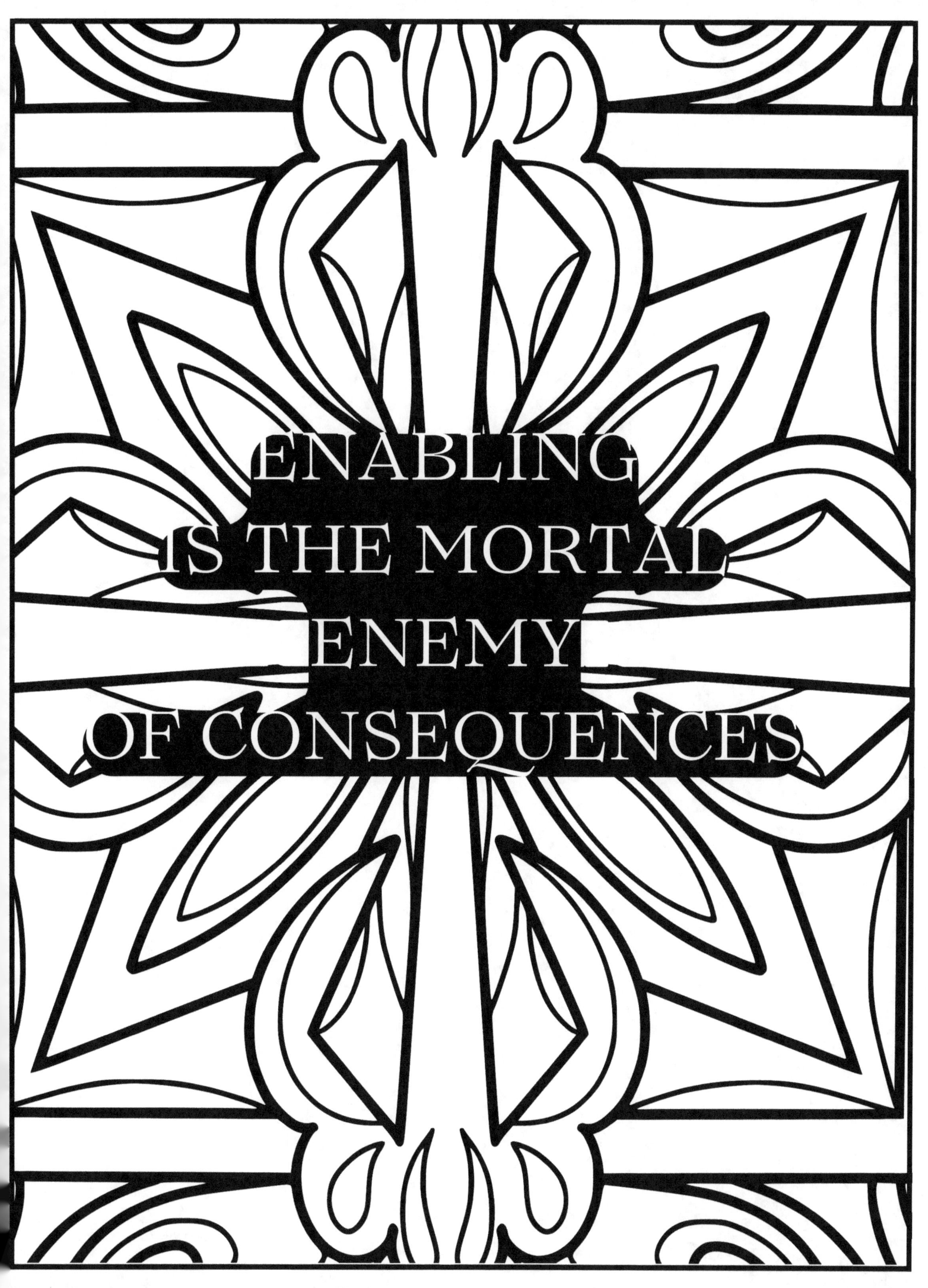
ENABLING
IS THE MORTAL
ENEMY
OF CONSEQUENCES

FAN

THE

FLAMES

OF

DESIRE

FOR

ATONEMENT

TO IGNITE

SOBRIETY

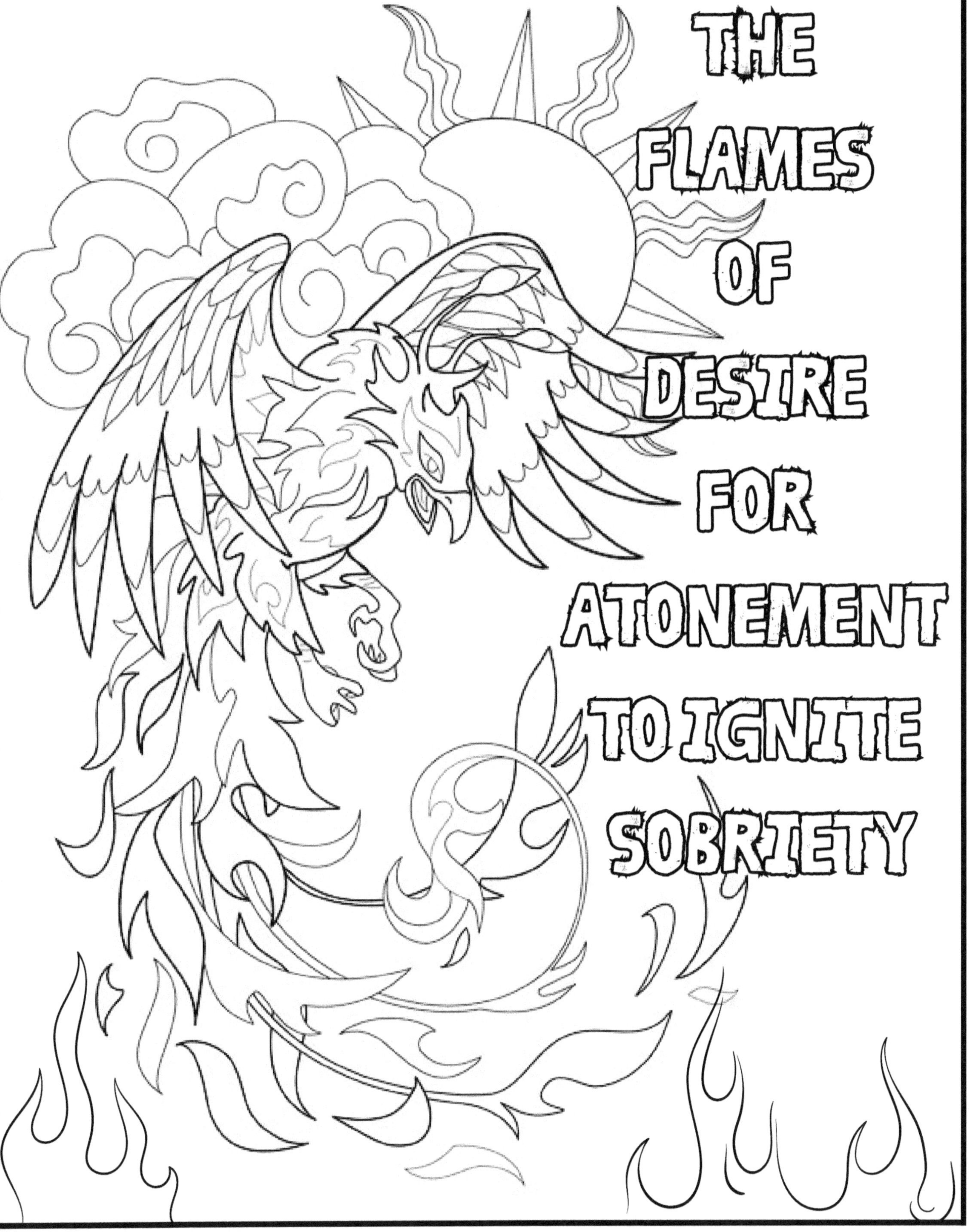

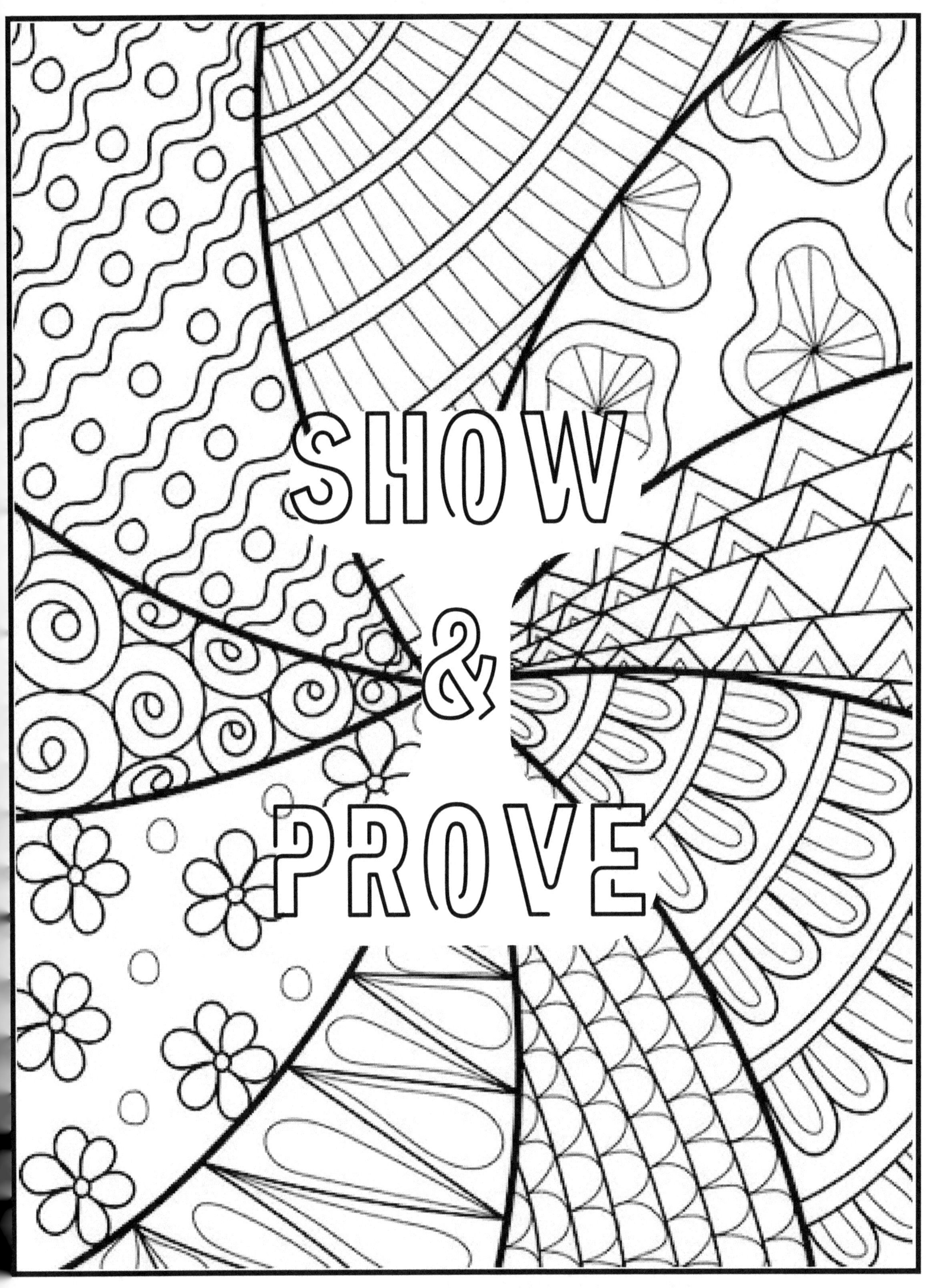
SHOW
&
PROVE

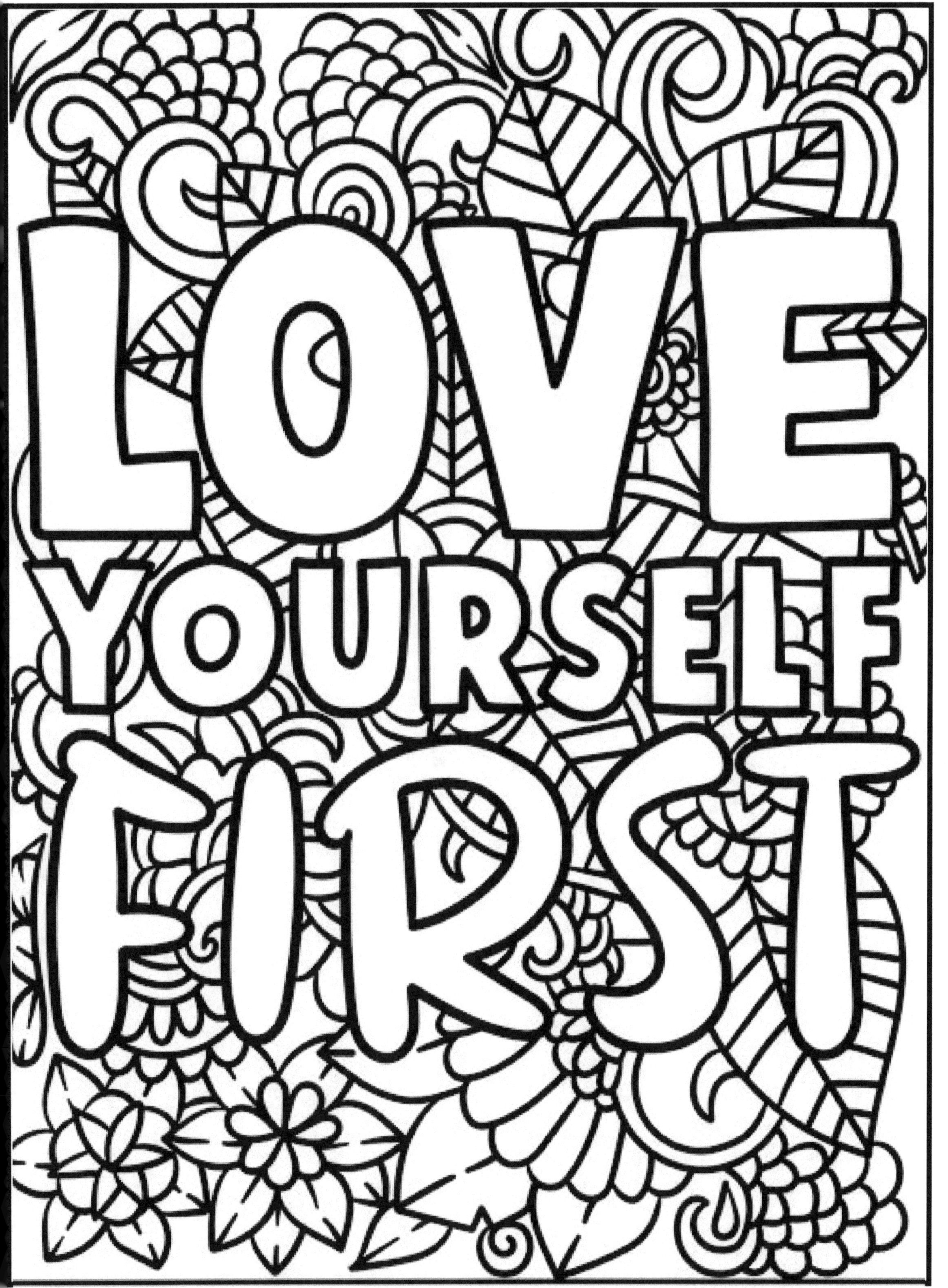
LOVE
YOURSELF
FIRST

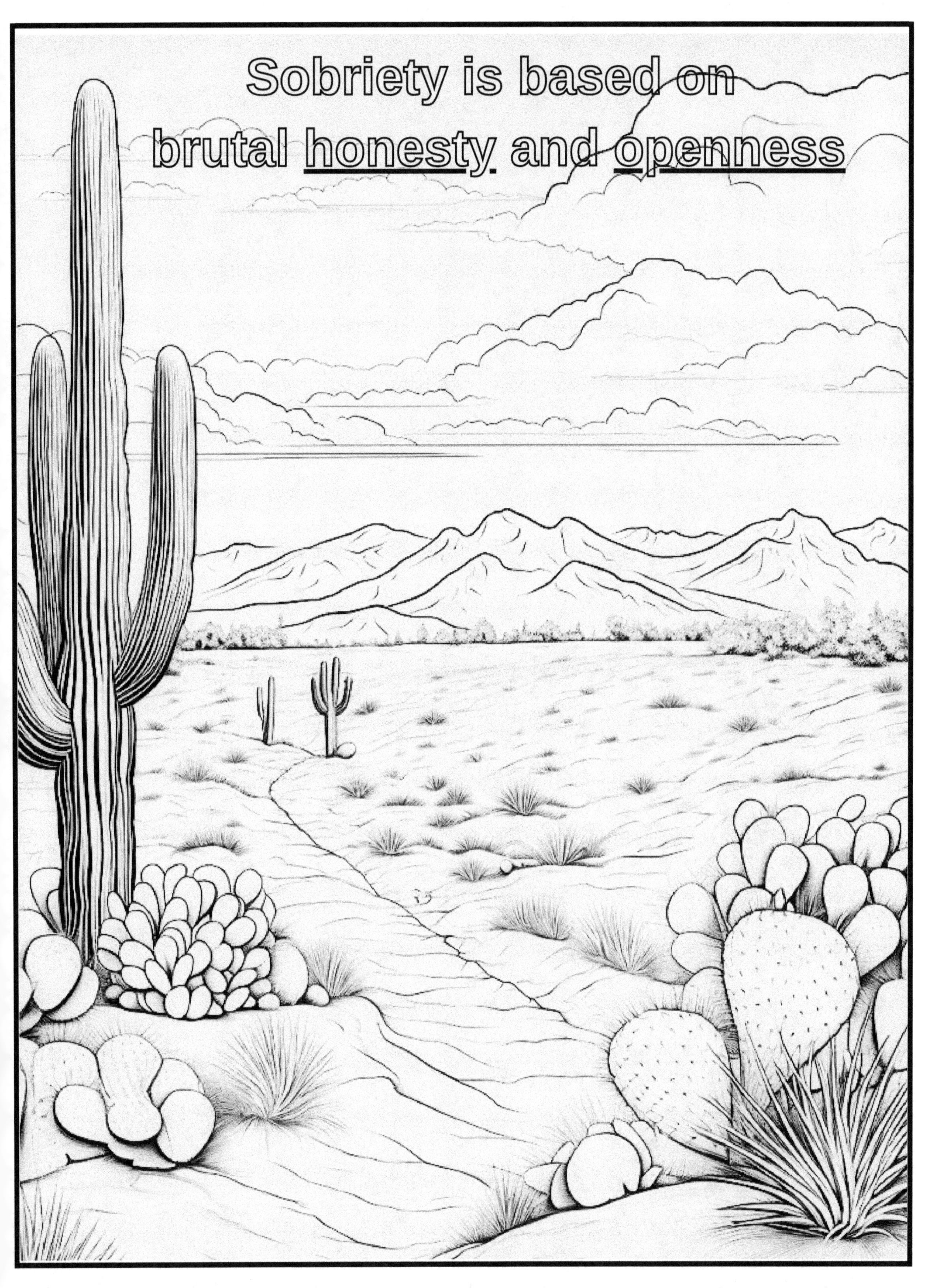
Sobriety is based on
brutal honesty and openness

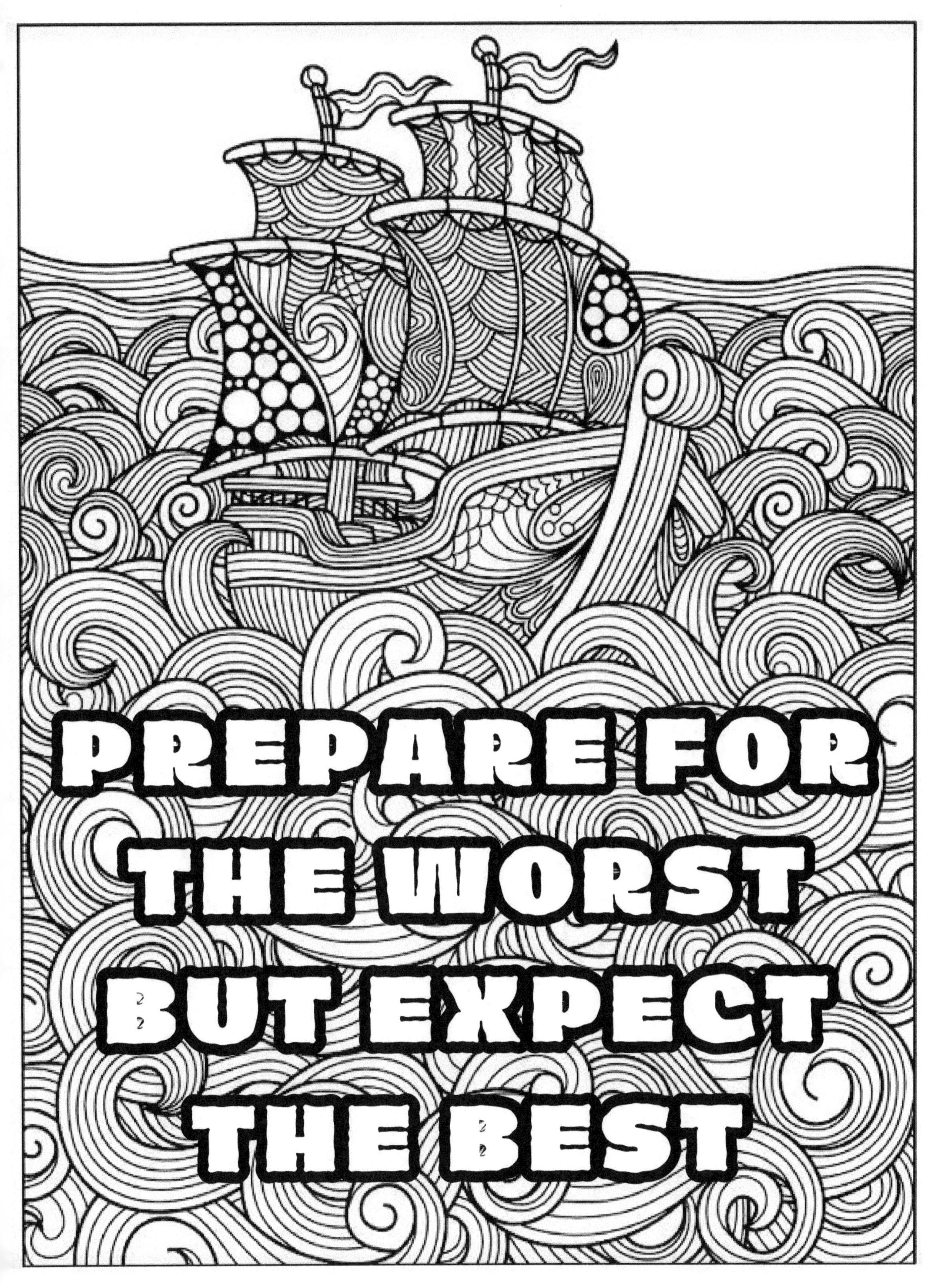
PREPARE FOR
THE WORST
BUT EXPECT
THE BEST

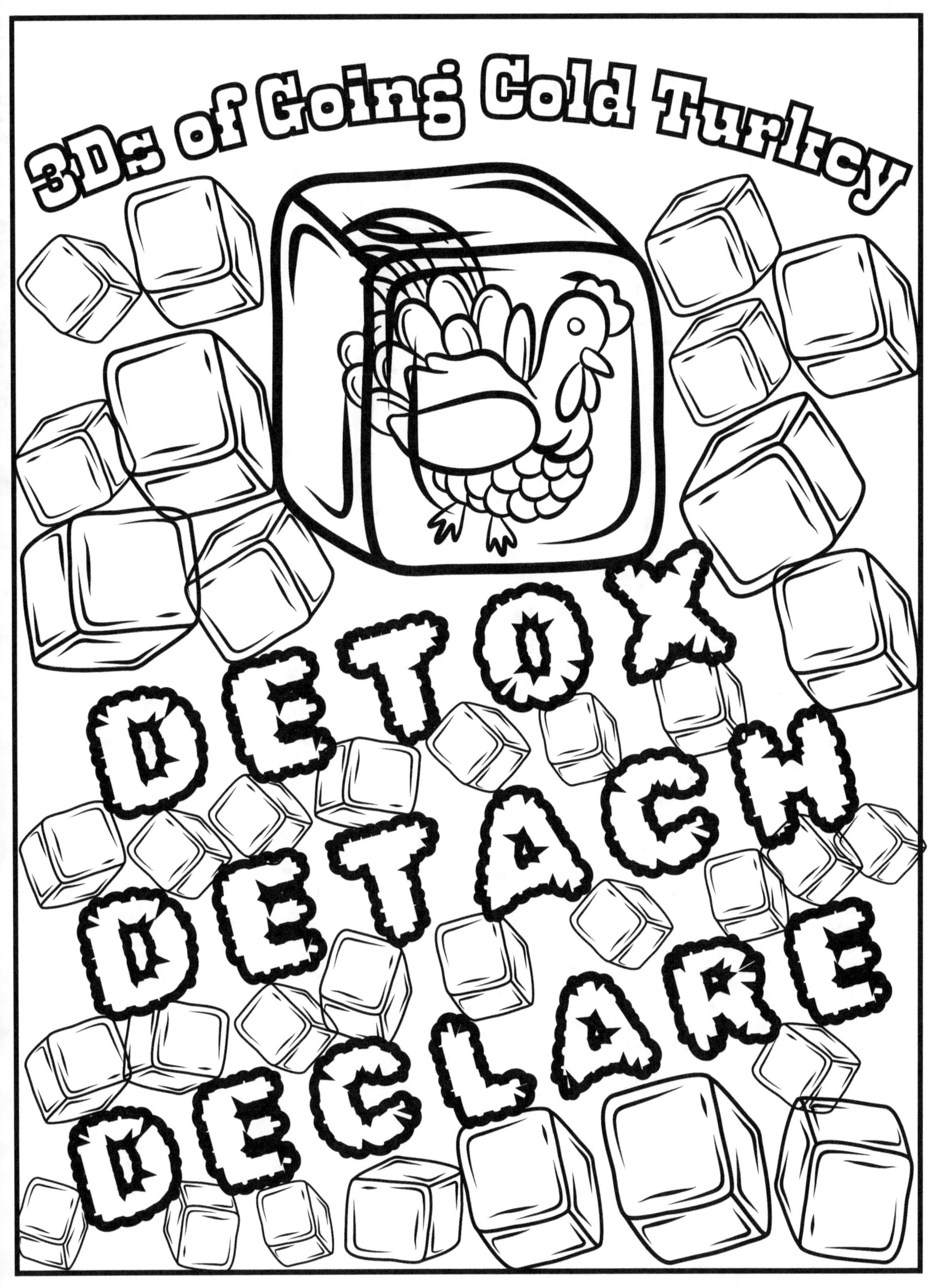
3Ds of Going Cold Turkey
DETOX
DETACH
DECLARE

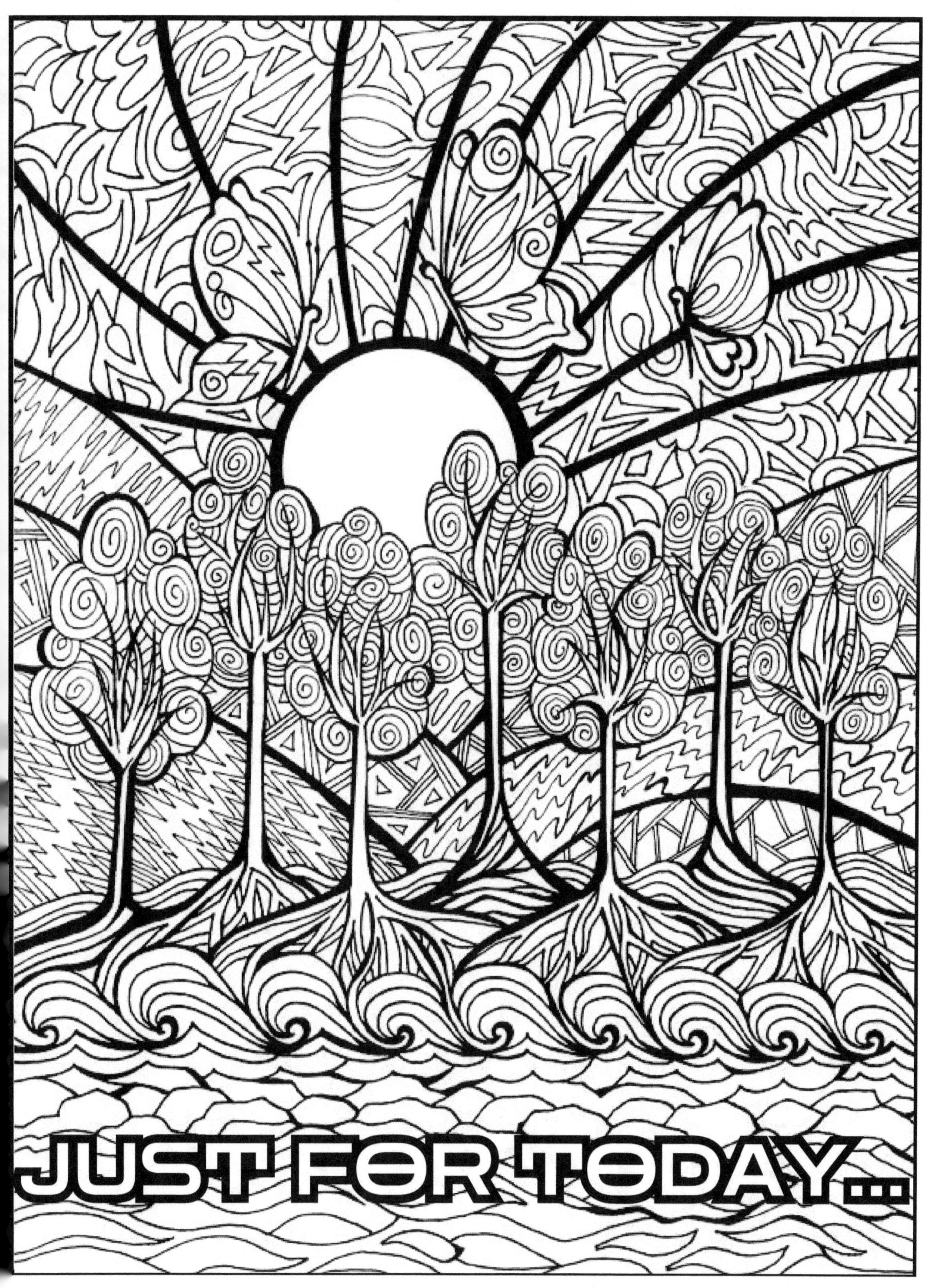
JUST FOR TODAY...

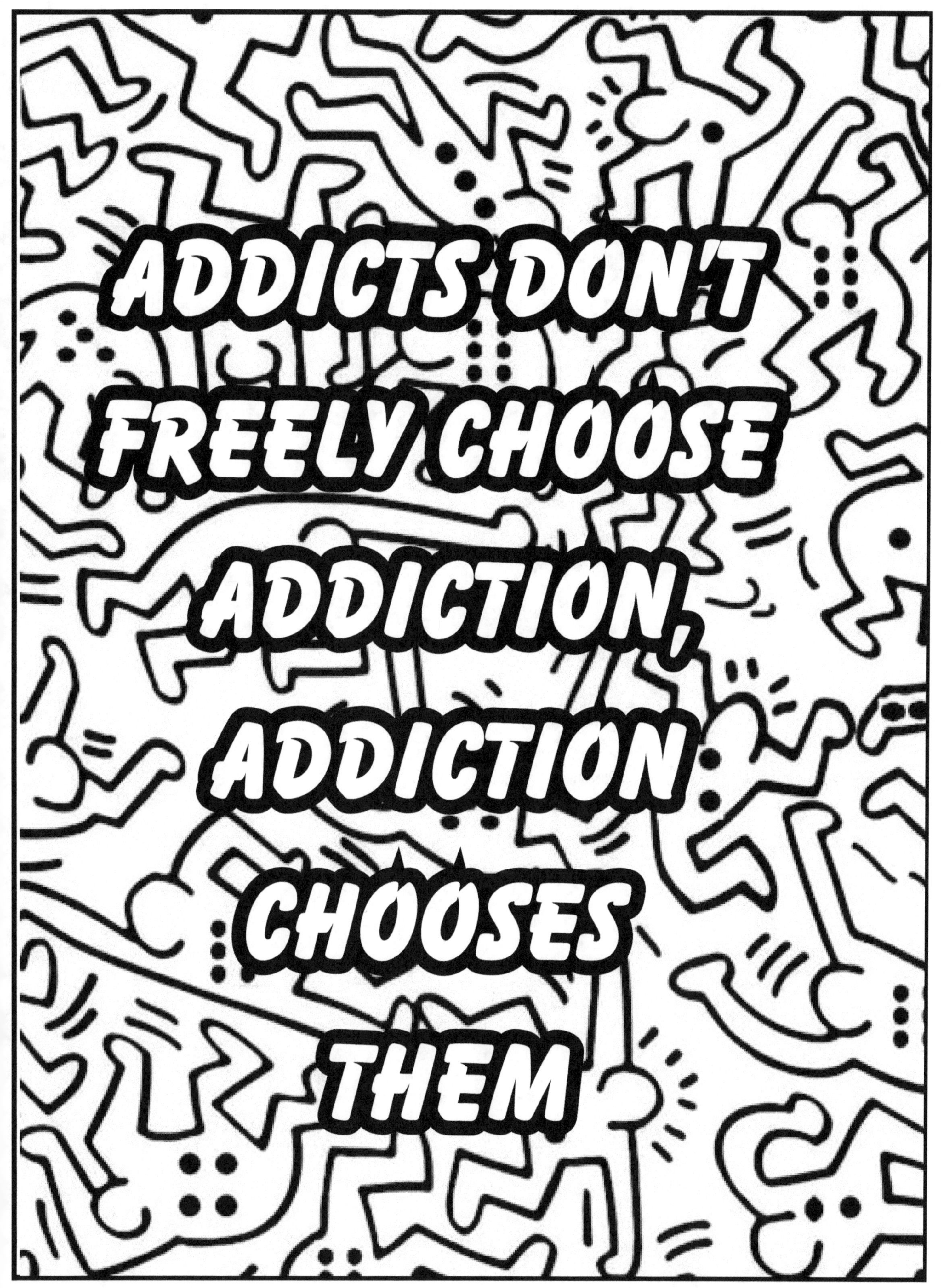
ADDICTS DON'T
FREELY CHOOSE
ADDICTION,
ADDICTION
CHOOSES
THEM

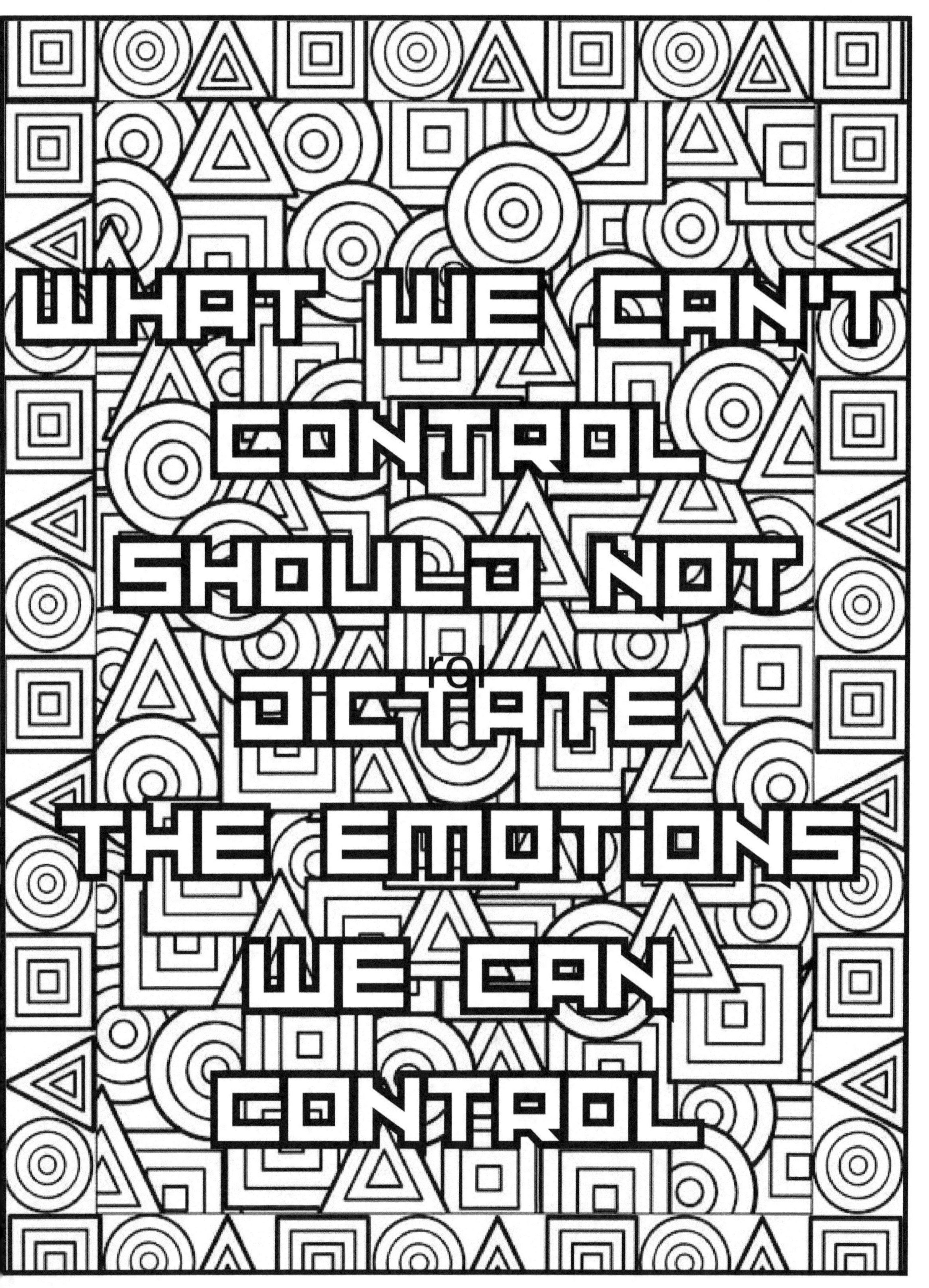
WHAT WE CAN'T
CONTROL
SHOULD NOT
DICTATE
THE EMOTIONS
WE CAN
CONTROL

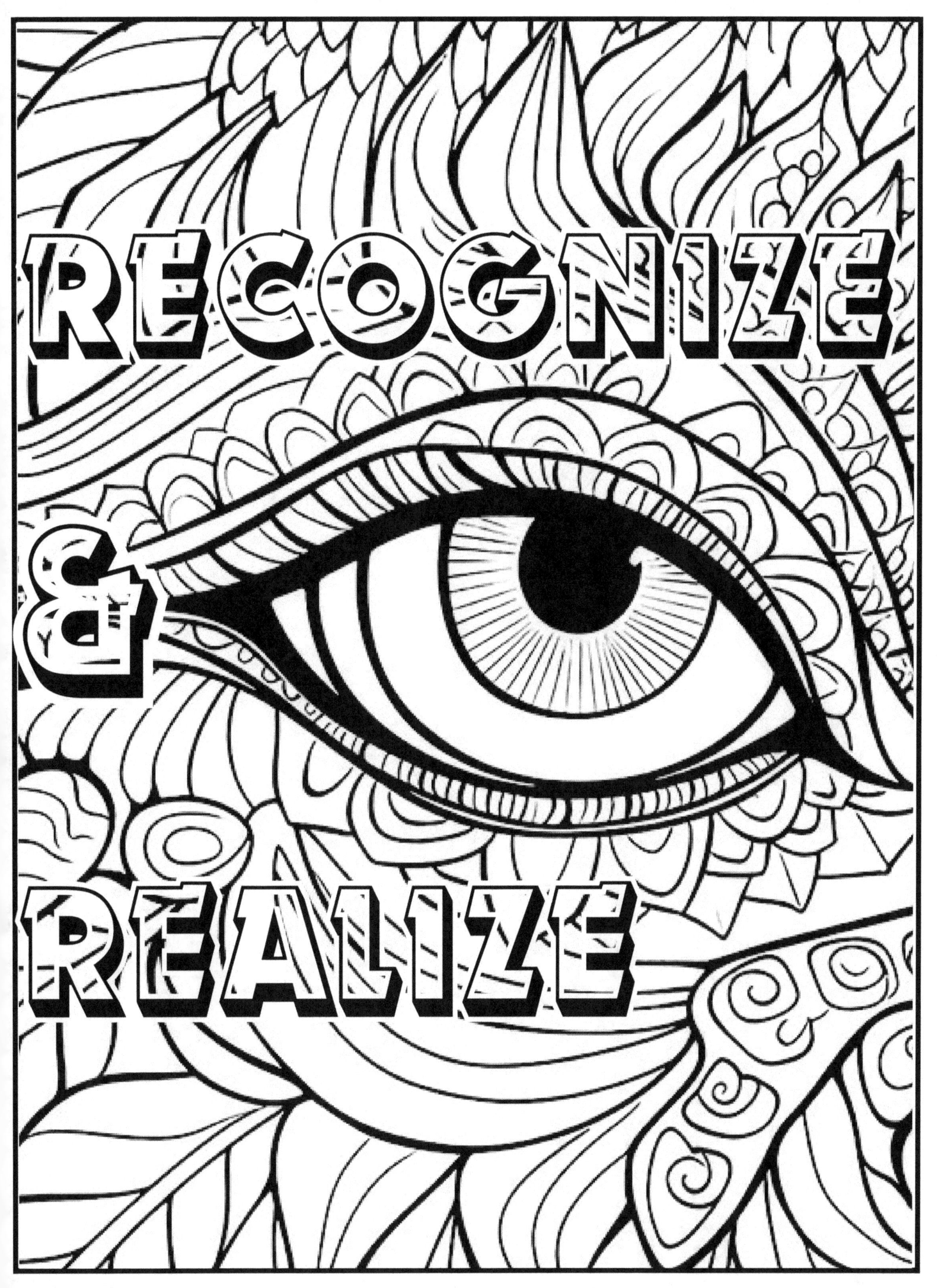
RECOGNIZE
&
REALIZE

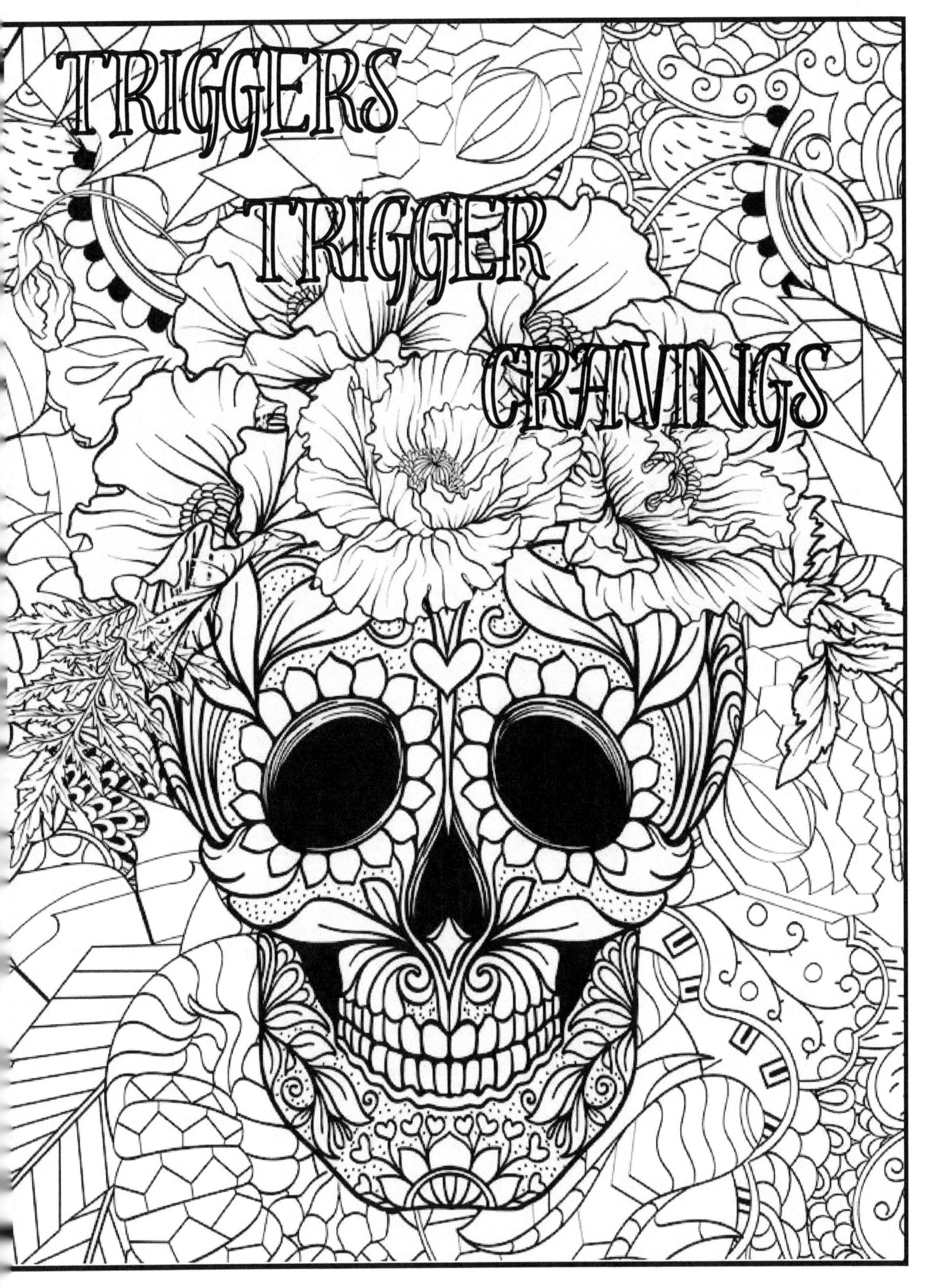
TRIGGERS
TRIGGER
CRAVINGS

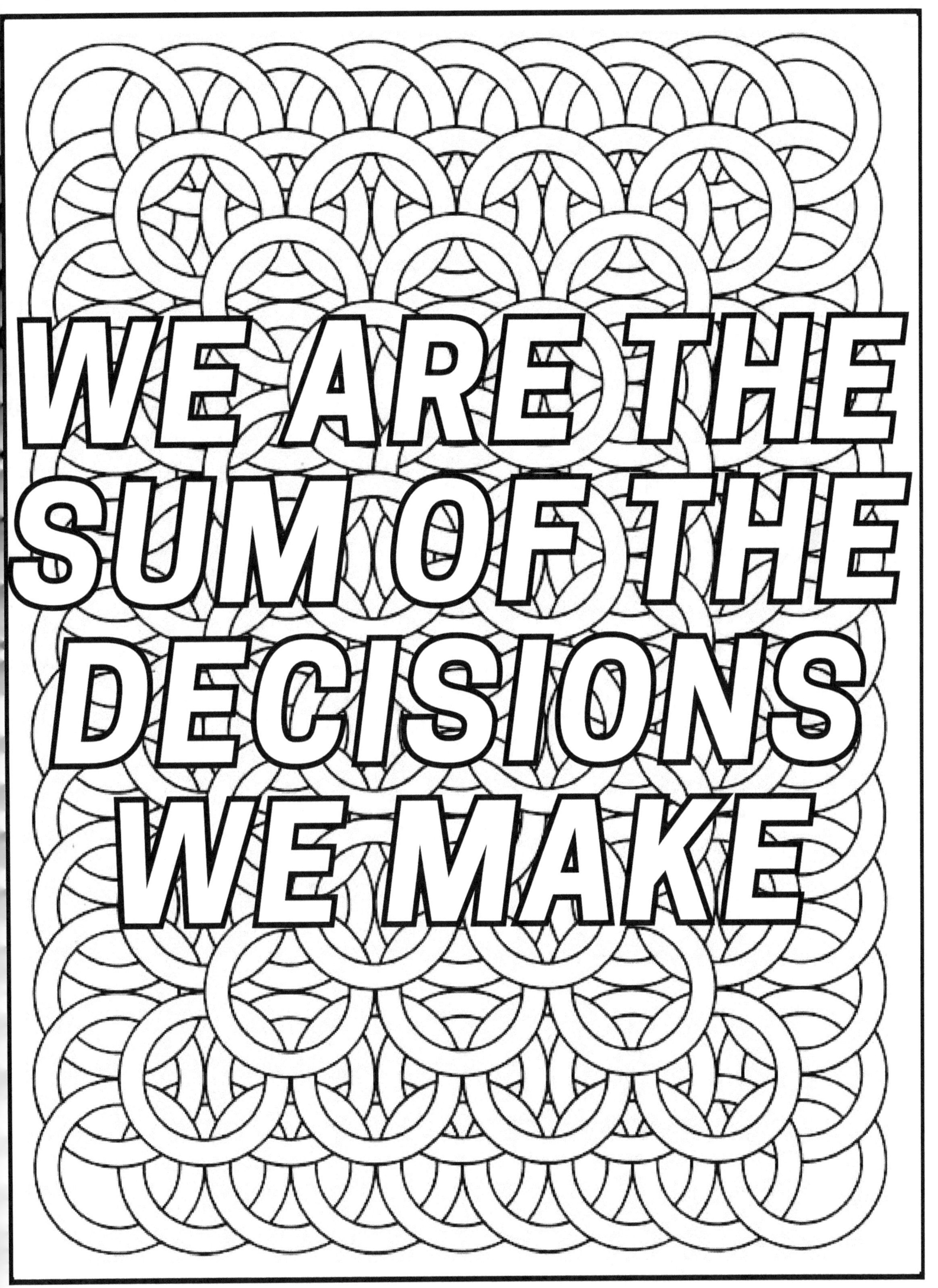
WE ARE THE
SUM OF THE
DECISIONS
WE MAKE

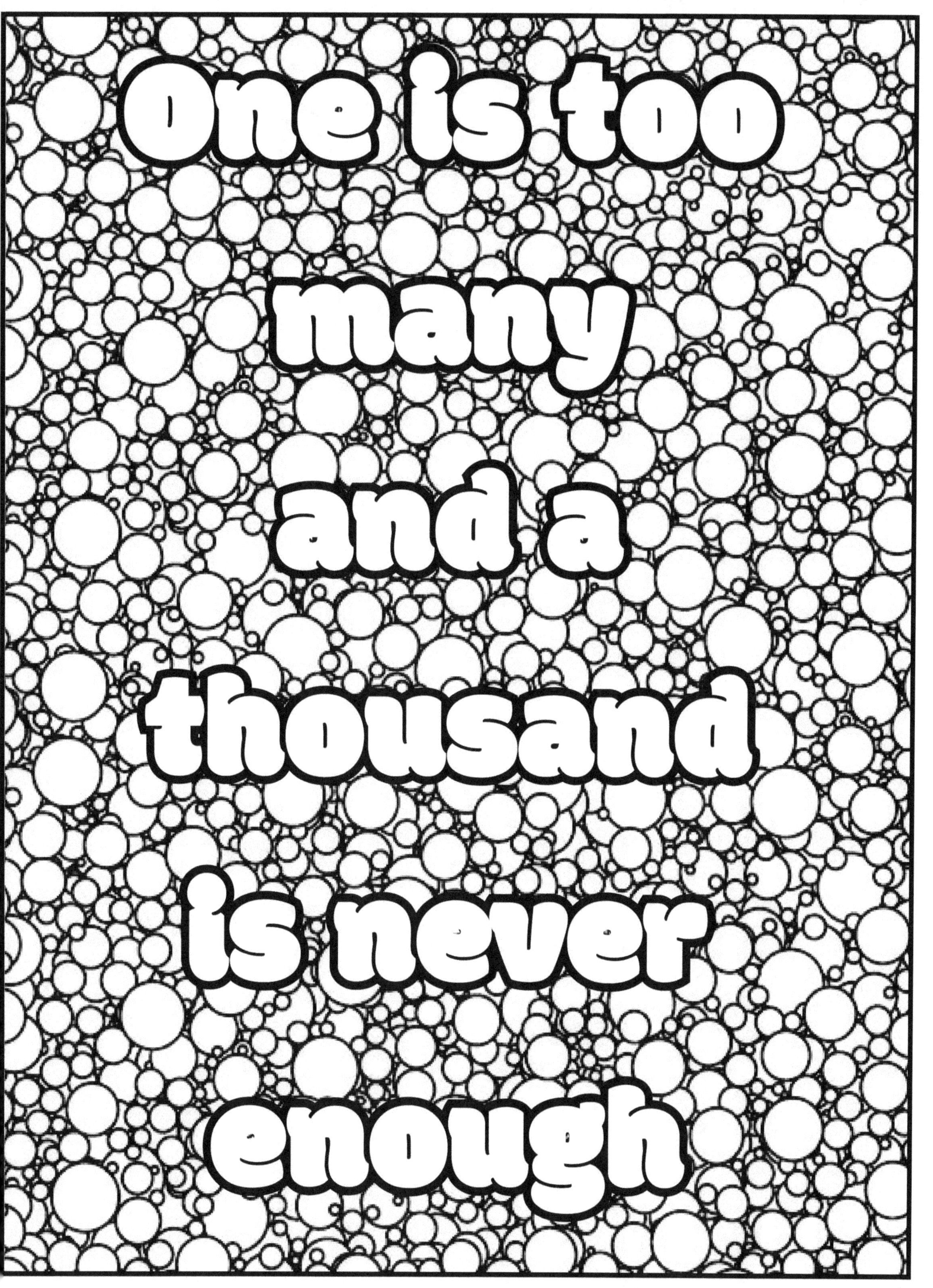
One is too
many
and a
thousand
is never
enough

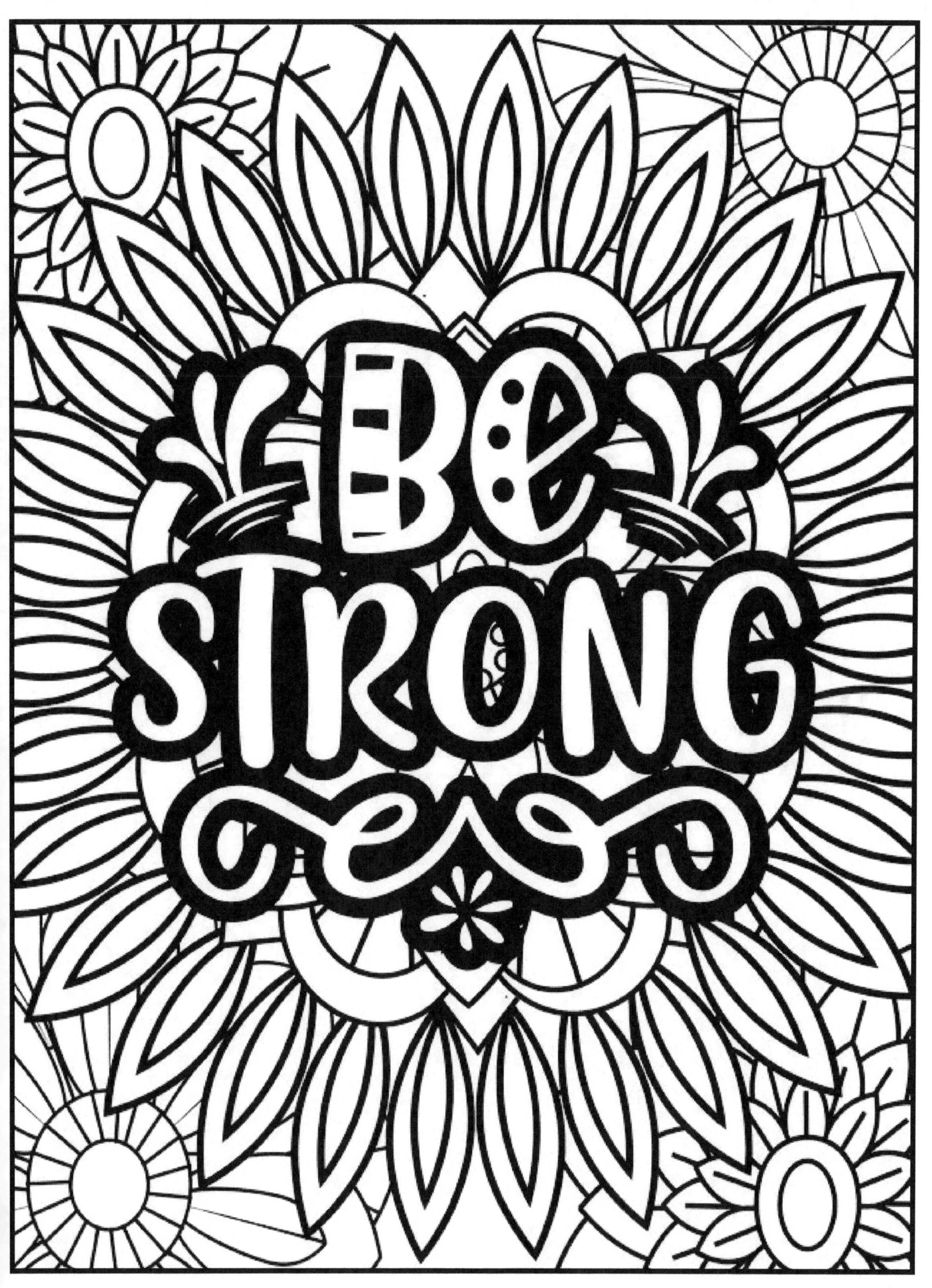
Be
STRONG

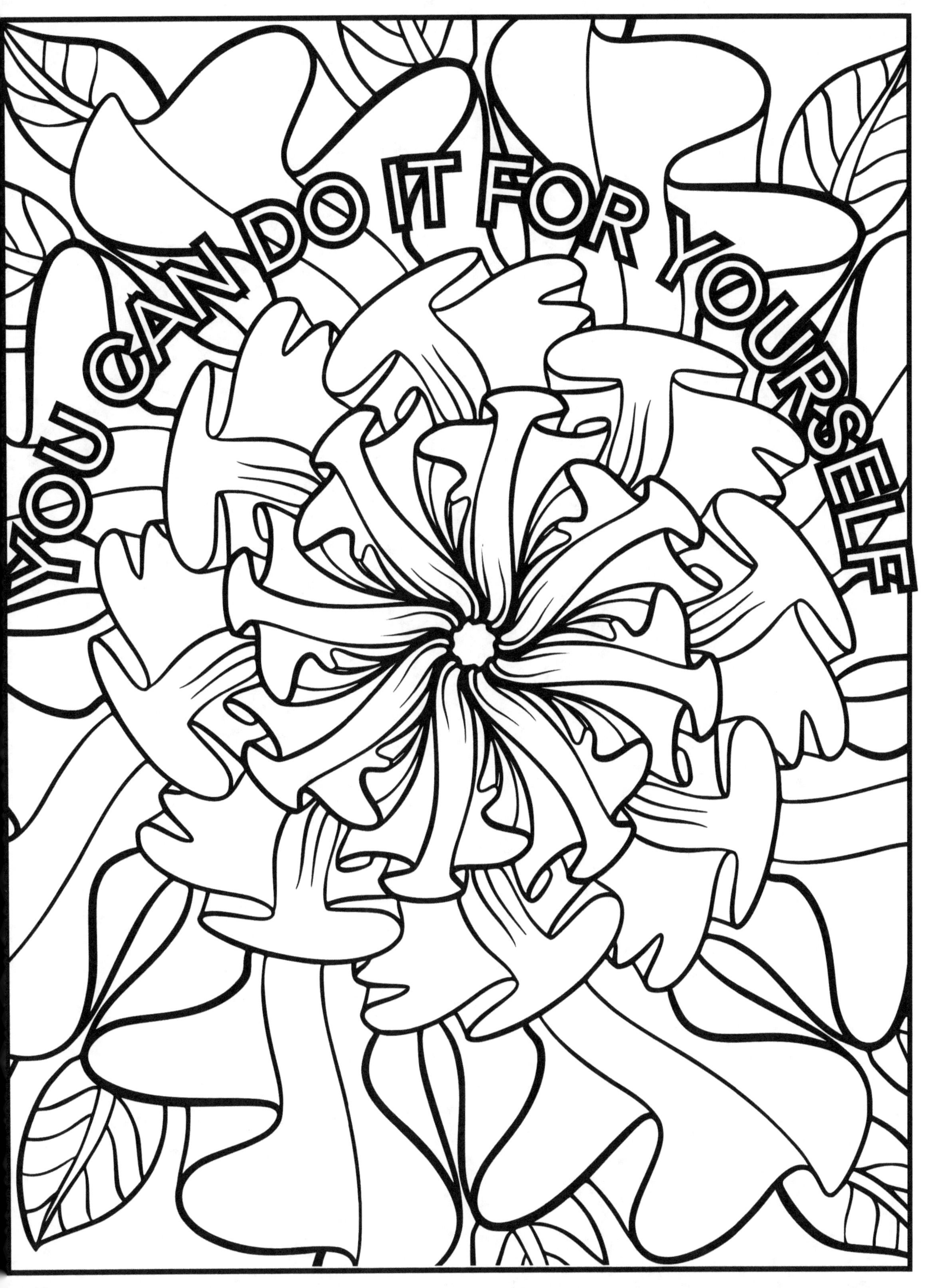
YOU CAN DO IT FOR YOURSELF

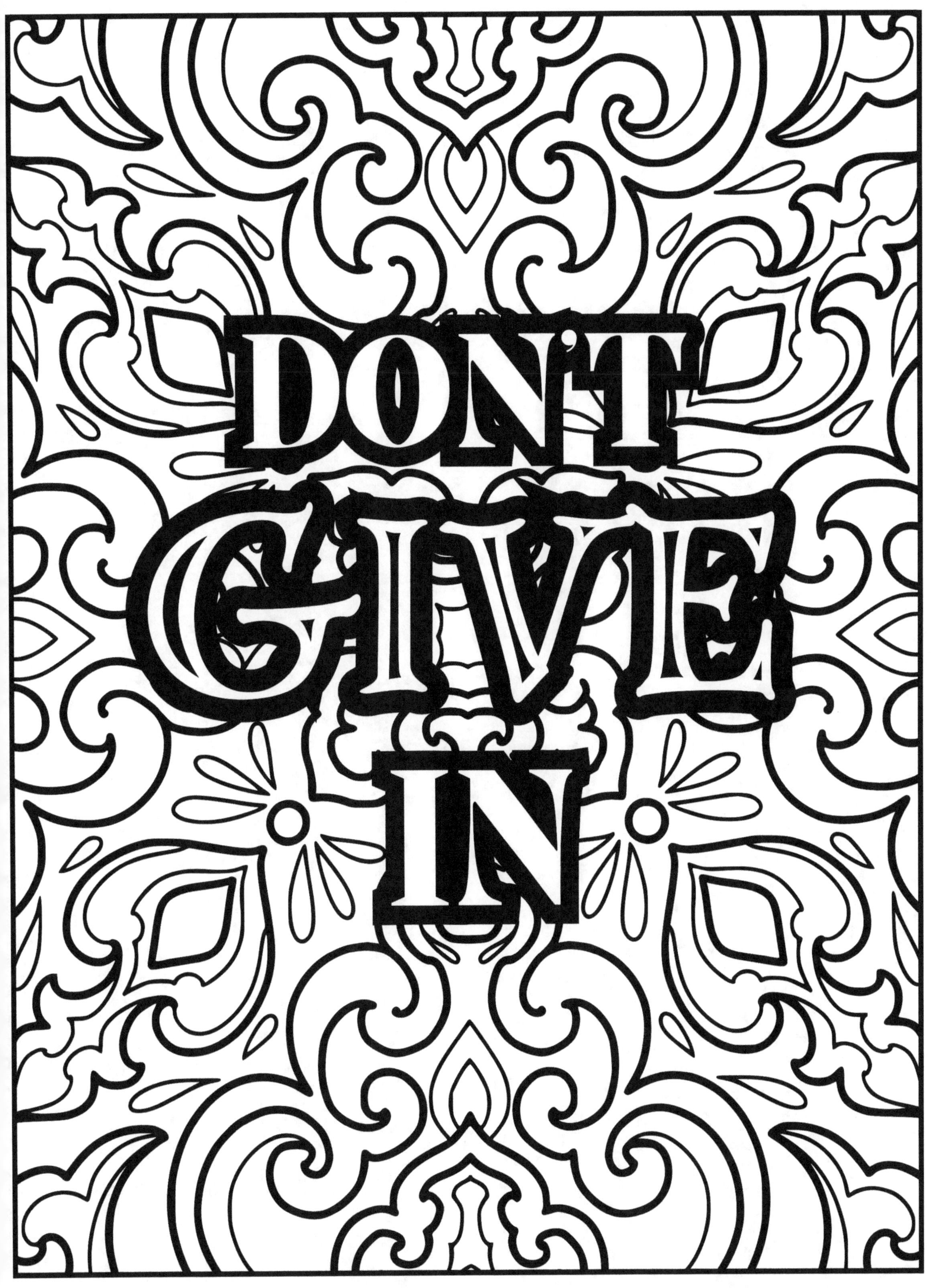
DON'T
GIVE
IN

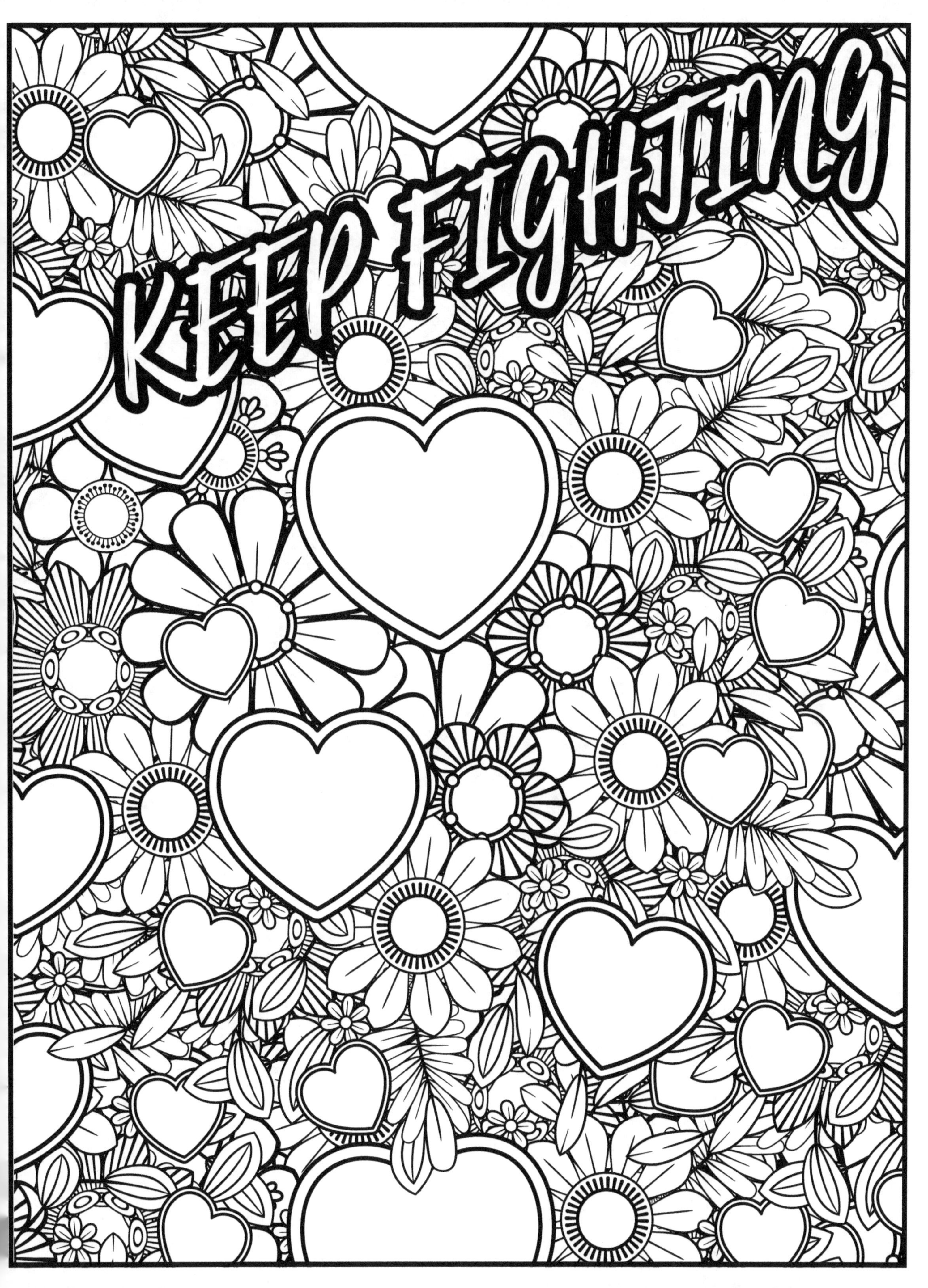
KEEP FIGHTING

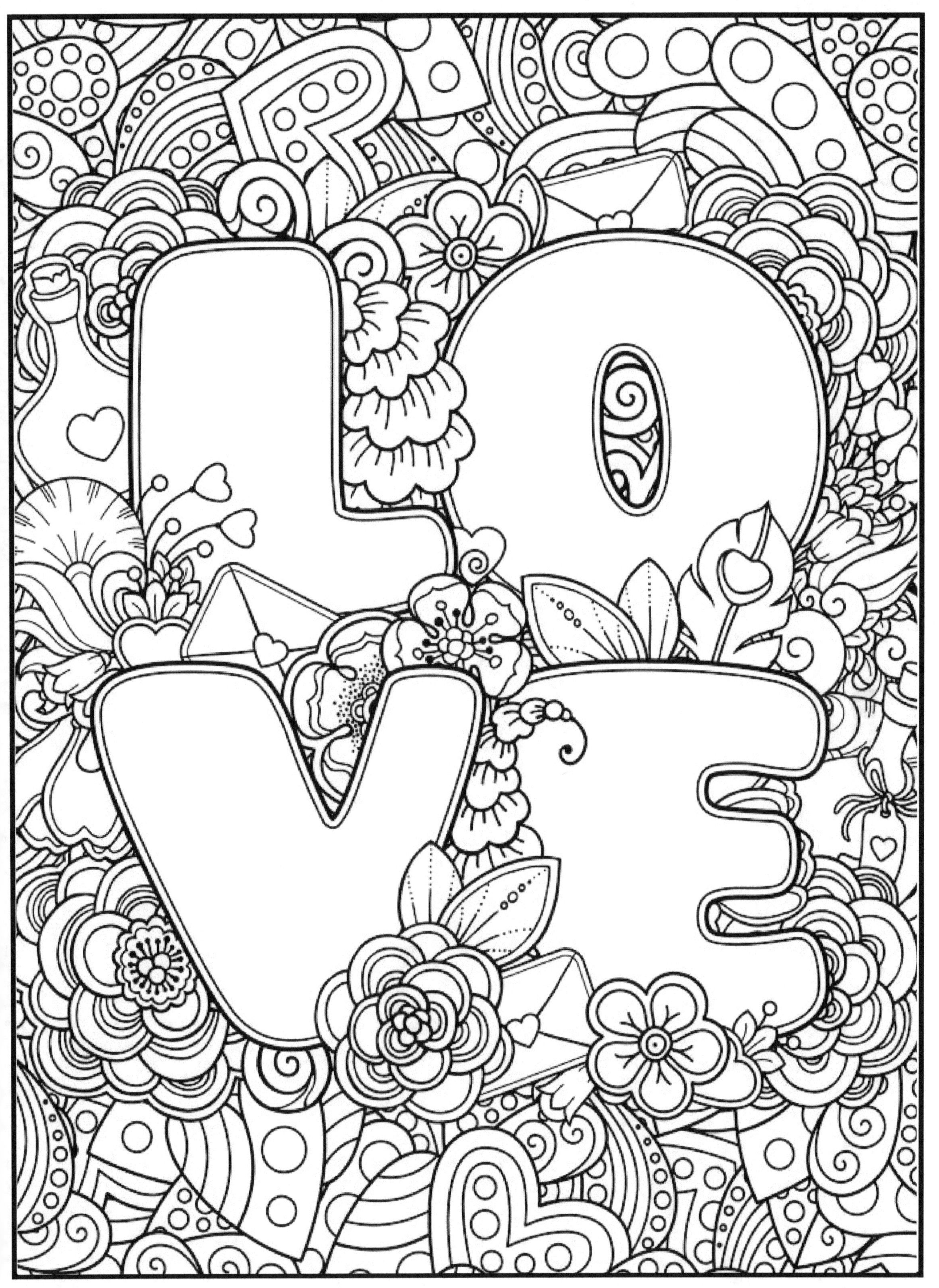
LOVE

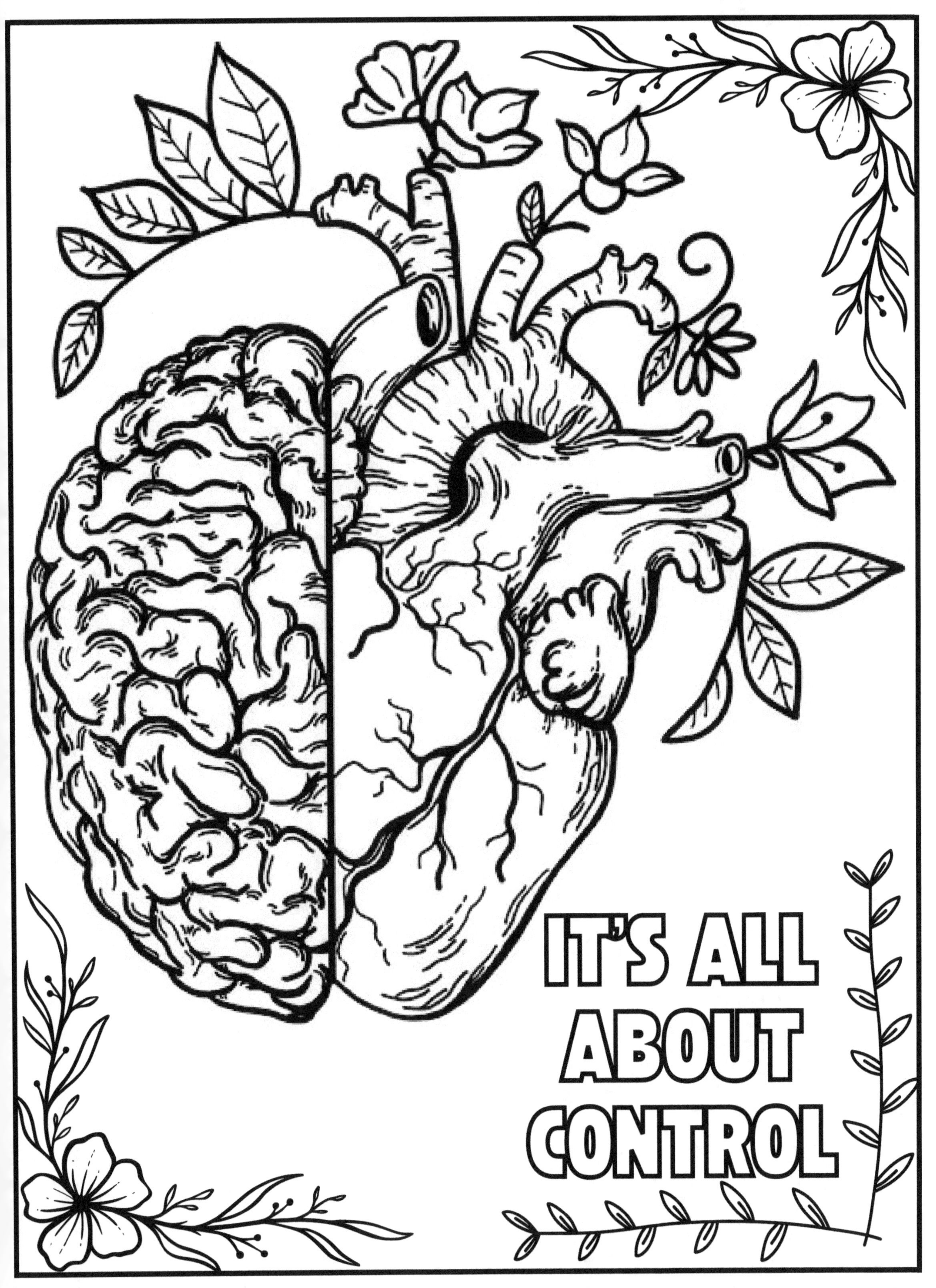
IT'S ALL ABOUT CONTROL

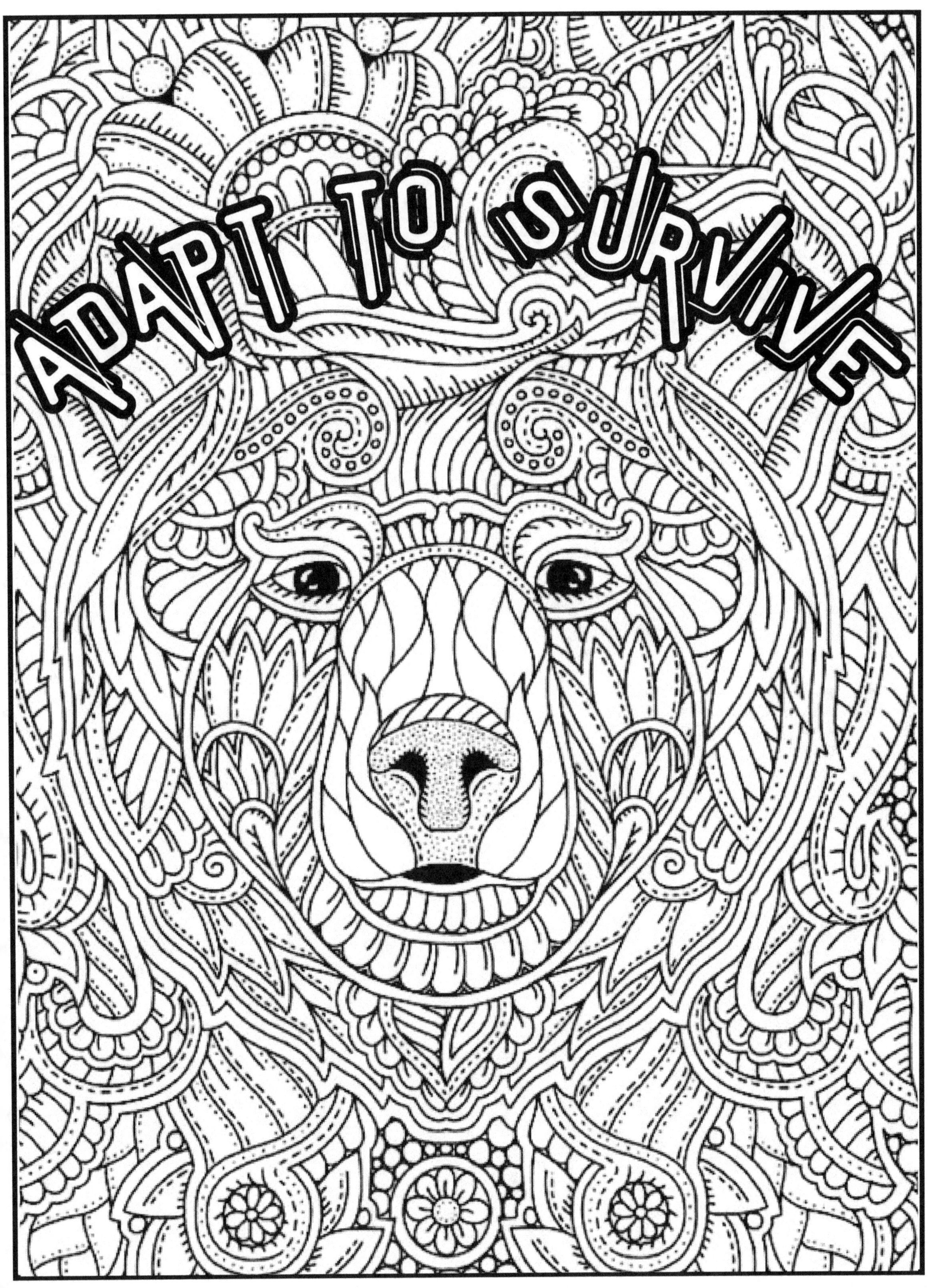
ADAPT TO SURVIVE

DC Hyden, M.A., M-CASAC

Addiction Clinician - Program Director - Author of:

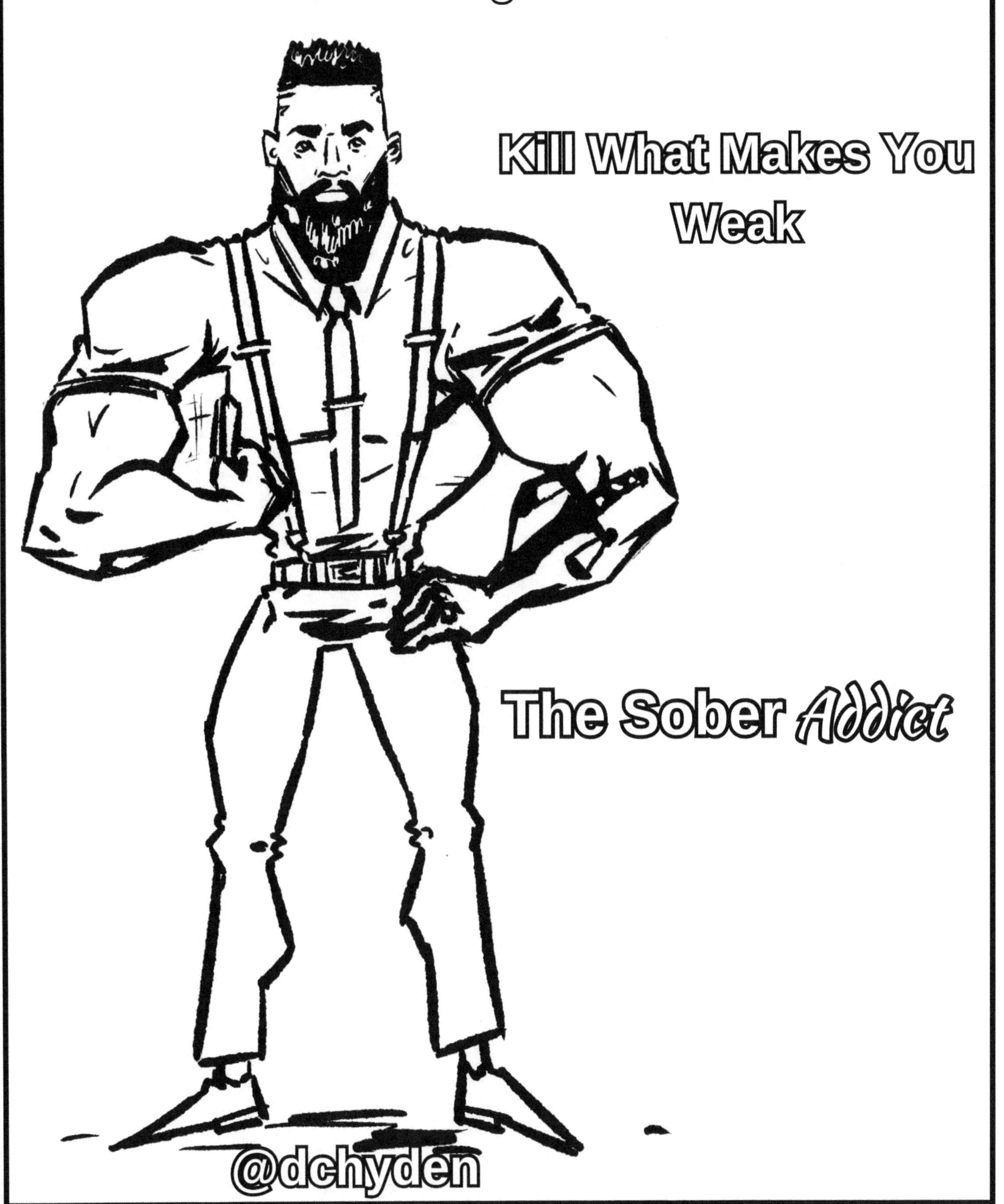

Kill What Makes You Weak

The Sober *Addict*

@dchyden

www.ingramcontent.com/pod-product-compliance
Lightning Source LLC
LaVergne TN
LVHW061253100826
845148LV00008B/1109

* 9 7 8 1 7 3 5 9 7 3 8 1 4 *